Plato and Popcorn

to
John Ellsworth Winter,
for all kinds of good reasons

Plato and Popcorn

A Philosopher's Guide to 75 Thought-Provoking Movies

WILLIAM G. SMITH

McFarland & Company, Inc., Publishers
Jefferson, North Carolina, and London

LIBRARY OF CONGRESS CATALOGUING-IN-PUBLICATION DATA

Smith, William G., 1943–
    Plato and popcorn : A philosopher's guide to 75
thought-provoking movies / William G. Smith.
      p.   cm.
    Includes bibliographical references and index.

    ISBN 0-7864-1878-8 (softcover : 50# alkaline paper) ∞

    1. Motion pictures — Plots, themes, etc.   I. Title.
PN1997.8.S63   2004
791.43'75 — dc22   2004008629

British Library cataloguing data are available

Cover: *Top photograph:* ©2004 Clipart.com. *Bottom photograph:*
Ewa Blaszczyk and Piotr Machalica in *Decalogue IX* (1988)

Manufactured in the United States of America

McFarland & Company, Inc., Publishers
  Box 611, Jefferson, North Carolina 28640
   www.mcfarlandpub.com

Contents

Preface   1

1. Did You Ever Think You Knew Something,
   but Didn't?   5
   Movie 1: *Twelve Angry Men*   9
   Movie 2: *The Return of Martin Guerre*   10
   Movie 3: *House of Games*   14
   Movie 4: *Rashomon*   16

2. The Greatest Happiness Principle   19
   Movie 5: *Abandon Ship*   23
   Movie 6: *The Field*   25

3. Doing One's Duty   27
   Movie 7: *High Noon*   29
   Movie 8: *The Road Home*   29

4. Anxiety and Inauthenticity   32
   Movie 9: *Hannah and Her Sisters*   33
   Movie 10: *My Dinner with Andre*   35
   Movie 11: *About Schmidt*   38

5. Fate and Determinism   42
   Movie 12: *Tess*   45
   Movie 13: *Sliding Doors*   46

6. Jesus, Muhammad, Buddha, Tammy Faye and
   Miscellaneous Religious Issues   48
   Movie 14: *The Last Temptation of Christ*   48
   Movie 15: *The Message*   51
   Movie 16: *Little Buddha*   53

Movie 17: *The Apostle*   55
Movie 18: *Breaking the Waves*   56
Movie 19: *The Eyes of Tammy Faye*   58
Movie 20: *The Decalogue*   59

7. The Journey Upward   67
Movie 21: *Billy Elliot*   69
Movie 22: *Girlfight*   70
Movie 23: *The Truman Show*   72
Movie 24: *The Matrix*   74
Movie 25: *The Color Purple*   78

8. Civil Disobedience   81
Movie 26: *Gattaca*   82
Movie 27: *Gandhi*   84

9. Death   87
Movie 28: *Shadowlands*   87
Movie 29: *Under the Sand*   89
Movie 30: *Fearless*   90
Movie 31: *Whose Life Is It Anyway?*   92
Movie 32: *Dead Man Walking*   94
Movie 33: *Resurrection*   96
Movie 34: *The Seventh Seal*   99

10. War   104
Movie 35: *The Red Badge of Courage*   105
Movie 36: *Paths of Glory*   106
Movie 37: *Saving Private Ryan*   108
Movie 38: *Full Metal Jacket*   109
Movie 39: *No Man's Land*   112

11. Racism   115
Movie 40: *The Birth of a Nation*   116
Movie 41: *Mississippi Burning*   117
Movie 42: *American History X*   119
Movie 43: *Do the Right Thing*   120
Movie 44: *The Long Walk Home*   122
Movie 45: *Imitation of Life*   123

12. The Holocaust 126
  Movie 46: *Shoah* 126
  Movie 47: *The Pianist* 129
  Movie 48: *Mr. Death* 130
  Movie 49: *Life Is Beautiful* 131

13. Sexism and Women's Issues 134
  Movie 50: *In the Company of Men* 137
  Movie 51: *Thelma and Louise* 138
  Movie 52: *Ladybird, Ladybird* 140
  Movie 53: *If These Walls Could Talk—Part I* 142
  Movie 54: *Real Women Have Curves* 144
  Movie 55: *Artemisia* 145
  Movie 56: *Whale Rider* 147
  Movie 57: *Daughters of the Dust* 148

14. Gay Rights 152
  Movie 58: *Chasing Amy* 153
  Movie 59: *If These Walls Could Talk—Part II* 155
  Movie 60: *Philadelphia* 156
  Movie 61: *The Celluloid Closet* 157

15. Pornography 161
  Movie 62: *The People vs. Larry Flynt* 162
  Movie 63: *The Pornographer* 164

16. Love, Love, Love 167
  Movie 64: *When Harry Met Sally* 167
  Movie 65: *East-West* 169
  Movie 66: *The Lover* 171
  Movie 67: *The Bridges of Madison County* 172
  Movie 68: *Sidewalks of New York* 173
  Movie 69: *Indecent Proposal* 174
  Movie 70: *Babette's Feast* 176
  Movie 71: *Pop and Me* 178

17. Puzzlers 183
  Movie 72: *The Usual Suspects* 183
  Movie 73: *Memento* 185
  Movie 74: *Mulholland Drive* 186

Contents

18. The Love of Movies   189
    Movie 75: *Cinema Paradiso*   189

    Notes   191
    Bibliography   195
    Index   199

Preface

You're going to have fun with the films covered in this book. Get ready to see 75 great movies and to think about them. Better yet — get some friends to join you in the quest. You're sure to have an intellectual feast!

There is nothing like seeing a good movie, one that is enjoyable both in itself and for the thought processes it stimulates. After all, it is good to think! Stretching the body with physical gymnastics develops a healthy body. This book will lead you through a series of intellectual gymnastics to help you strengthen your critical thinking abilities. Strong body, strong mind. What more can you ask?

At this point, you are probably wondering who is this guy who is going to lead me through 75 movies. Well, even if you are not wondering, I'm going to tell you. (1) I'm a movie lover. (2) I'm a professor of philosophy at the oldest state-owned university in Pennsylvania. (3) I like Ireland, classical music, and the Philadelphia Flyers ice hockey team. (4) I have two great children, but since they've "flown the coop," I have to search to fill the void. The result: I worked on this book and took up golf.

Let's talk about movies. None of the movies covered in this book are bad movies. Well, maybe two are, but even those two are thought-provoking. A few may not "speak" to you. Neither the *Mona Lisa* nor jazz speaks to me, but they are certainly not bad things. (I never could see the half-smile, half-frown on *Mona Lisa*. And the background of that painting looks, to me, like something from a cheap photography studio.)

Don't get me wrong. There *are* bad movies. And some movies are better than others. *Raiders of the Lost Ark* is a better film than *Indiana Jones and the Temple of Doom*. The former is a fine fantasy adventure film in which Indiana Jones escapes from dangerous situations in ways that do not damage our reasoning capacity. A huge boulder chases him

1

through a cave. He is trapped in a snake-filled pit. His escapes are com-patible with the laws of nature. But turn to *Indiana Jones and the Temple of Doom* and what happens? Indiana Jones and a female companion are in a plane that is going to crash. No parachute. How do they escape? They jump out of the plane with an inflatable life raft! The inflated raft floats down, lands on the top of a snow-covered mountain, slides down the mountain to a river and floats peacefully downstream. There should be an additional rating: "BD" for "this movie could be hazardous to your intellectual health — it could cause *brain death*!"

A type of "BD" movie is the "ka-ka movie." Such movies appeal to most adolescents and to many "adults." Scenes of "shooting the moon" send scores of people into hysterics. Even *Jurassic Park* contains too many "ka-ka" elements. A man runs into an outhouse to hide from a dinosaur. The dinosaur swings his tail, smashing the outhouse. The only thing that remains is the man sitting on the pot. Characters find a pile of dinosaur manure and one says, "That's a big pile of shit." (More hysterical laugh-ter.) In *Lethal Weapon II*, Danny Glover is sitting on the commode. If he gets up, a bomb goes off. Mel Gibson helps him get away, but the bomb still goes off. The toilet is not destroyed, but rather flies through the air and lands on a police car. (Ha, ha, ha.) BD.

Before I sound too much like a prude, I will admit that I, too, some-times enjoy BD movies. Seeing Mary with that stuff in her hair in *There's Something About Mary* was funny. However, human beings cannot live on BD alone. Many of my students question whether judgments of movies being "better" or "worse" are mere statements of opinion. My view: if all one sees are BD movies, then one's judgments would be mere statements of opinion. However, there *are* better judges than those who only see BD movies.

So why did I write this book? Because I am a missionary for good movies, and because I have experienced the joys of discussing many of them with close acquaintances. Exciting discussions also arise in my "Phi-losophy in Film" classes and after the showing of films to our Philoso-phy Club. I want you, the reader, to have such exciting thoughts and discussions.

This book presents 75 movies, which are divided into 18 categories. After reading my introductory comments the reader should view the movie. Then the reader should turn to the questions I raise. These questions will stimulate thought about the movie. (Of course, the reader will easily generate his or her own questions.)

Some may have difficulty finding a particular DVD or video. At the end of most chapters I list additional recommendations of movies that deal with themes covered. These movies can be used as substitutes for the ones listed.

One other thing: some movies covered shouldn't offend anyone; others, however, may contain explicit violence, sexual scenes, or very nasty characters. I will provide some warning for those who would like to be forewarned about material that may be offensive.

Never read the questions I raise for discussion before watching the movie; they will give away too much of the plot. I've found that the best way to view a film is to know as little about it as possible. Too many reviewers merely summarize the plot — that is the easy and lazy way to review a movie. I've developed the technique of looking at a review and only seeing what the reviewer generally thought of the movie. I blank out when the plot is disclosed. I recommend that you do the same.

How do you find a DVD or video when your local video store doesn't have it? Search for "movie rentals" on the Internet. It is surprisingly easy to find movies that can be sent to your house, complete with easy instructions on how to return them. Here are a few websites I recommend:

www.facets.org
www.netflix.com
www.bestvideo.com
www.reel.com

There are many ways to purchase DVDs or videos. One of the best sources is deepdiscountdvd.com. Also good is amazon.com.

A lot of credit for any good ideas in this book must go to a number of special friends. Donna Kilhefner worked tirelessly at putting the manuscript in final form, and in providing helpful suggestions along the way. Matt Johnson, a student, proofread the entire manuscript for me. Matt knows so much about film history that *I* am often *his* student. He was particularly helpful in providing insight into exactly what happens in *Mulholland Drive* (Movie 74). My long-time friend Gus Meckley is the person with whom I have seen more movies than anyone else. We've traveled many, many miles, many, many times to see films that wouldn't come to our local theaters. Discussions with Gus provided me with many of the ideas expressed in this book. Colleagues who provided useful information when I had questions were Jack Fischel, Jen Miller, and Jill Craven. Bartosz Zytkowiak, another student, introduced me to Kieslowski's *The Decalogue* (Movie 20). Linda Sheets typed early drafts of a number of chapters. My son Jason shares my love of movies. Though separated by many miles, as soon as either of us sees a new film, we get on the telephone to provide a critical assessment for the other. Jason's excitement for movies started when he was very young. He wanted so much to see *An American Werewolf in London*. I took him, but only on the condition that he put his head down during the scary parts. My daughter Tess is also partially responsible for my writing this book. Had she stayed a little girl, I would not have had to look for a new challenge. But she went to college. Last, but not least, I owe thanks to Millersville University of Pennsylvania for its support and intellectual climate.

Several of the movies covered in this book were introduced to me by Harlan Jacobson's "Talk Cinema." Harlan has set up Talk Cinema centers in a number of cities, including Philadelphia, New York, Boston, Dallas, and Chicago. Harlan regularly supplies movies of the highest quality. Members never know what movie they will view. After the film, an expert leads a discussion. Check out www.talkcinema.com.

1

Did You Ever Think You Knew Something, but Didn't?

The skeptical philosophy of David Hume (1711–1776) provides a wonderful foundation for thinking about the first four movies covered here. Summaries of three of Hume's arguments against claims that one can have knowledge of worldly matters are provided.

Argument No. 1: "All ideas are copies of impressions."

In his *Enquiry Concerning Human Understanding* Hume tries to prove that "all our ideas are copies of our impressions."[1] Impressions are perceptions that are "lively." An impression is perceived whenever a person "hears, or sees, or feels, or loves, or hates, or desires, or wills."[2] When one thinks about what one heard, saw, and felt or when one thinks about the psychological states of loving, hating, desiring, or willing, one is aware of an *idea*. Ideas are never as "lively" nor as "vivid" as the impressions they copy. As Hume put it: "The most lively thought is still inferior to the dullest sensation."[3]

If Hume is correct that all ideas are copies of impressions, and if he is correct that humans can never be exposed to anything but ideas and impressions, skepticism follows. Why? Ask yourself where impressions exist. Then ask yourself where ideas exist. The answer in both cases is *in the mind*. If all we can know are impressions and ideas, and if both are "in the mind," then we can not know anything about the world outside the mind. We are caught in what has been called " the egocentric predicament."

Add to the above that the sources of our ideas are the fallible senses and one is on the road to skepticism.

Argument No. 2: The Analytic/Synthetic Distinction

According to Hume, there are two — and only two — kinds of sentences: "relations of ideas" and "matters of fact."[4] Since the time of the great philosopher Immanuel Kant, relations of ideas have been called "analytic sentences" and matters of fact have been called "synthetic sentences." Since Kant's labels now are more common than Hume's, I will use Kant's. However, the reasoning I will present is that of Hume.

If Hume is right that the only possible types of sentences are analytic and synthetic sentences, skepticism follows. Why? In order to understand the answer to that question, one must first be clear about the nature of analytic and synthetic sentences. Analytic sentences have the following characteristics:

(a) "They are discoverable by the mere operation of thought, without dependence on what is anywhere existent in the universe."[5]

(b) They are necessarily true.

(c) They do not convey any information about reality.

(d) Nothing is thought in the predicate that is not already thought in the subject.

(e) If you deny an analytic sentence you contradict yourself.

Examples of analytic sentences are:

A. A square has four sides.

B. A rose is a rose.

C. A unicorn is a one-horned creature.

D. A million-headed King of France has many heads.

In A, if you think of a square you are already thinking of a four-sided figure. By merely thinking about any of the sentences A through D, you become aware that they are necessarily true. If you deny C, for example, you will contradict yourself. If you say, "A unicorn is not a one-horned creature," a contradiction arises since a unicorn (uni-horn) *is* a one-horned creature. You would be saying, "A one-horned creature is not a one-horned creature." However, no analytic sentence conveys information about the world. Example A does not tell you there are squares, any more than D establishes the existence of a million-headed King of France.

Synthetic sentences, on the other hand, have the following characteristics:

(a) To verify, or falsify, a synthetic sentence one must check to see how the world is.

(b) They are not necessarily true.

(c) They purportedly convey information about the world.

(d) The predicate is not thought when the subject is thought. (There is an attempted *synthesis* of two different concepts.)

(e) If you deny synthetic sentences no contradiction arises.

Examples of synthetic sentences are:

A. Lee Harvey Oswald assassinated John F. Kennedy.
B. George W. Bush is a male.
C. No coelacanth exists.
D. The author of this book is William Gerald Smith.

You would probably claim that at least B in the above list is true. However, your confidence in B can be shaken if you think about C. For years and years it was firmly believed coelacanths were extinct. However, that firm belief was shattered when one was caught in a Japanese fishing net. "George W. Bush is a male" could also be false! Have you looked to determine whether or not such is the case? Even if you have looked (strange!), have you ever heard of Velcro?! "But," you say, "that's silly!" Perhaps. However, then think of the women who, forbidden to serve as soldiers in the American Civil War, dressed like men so they could fight. Comrades were certain they were men. But eventually a few were discovered. Or consider Billy Tipton, the great jazz musician who died in 1989. Members of his band never knew he was a female. Her adopted son never knew. The public never knew. Why did she pass herself off as a male? One motive might lie in the fact that women have great difficulty making it in the male-dominated jazz world. Well, isn't it possible that Georgina W. Bush, knowing it was difficult for a woman to win election in a male-dominated political world, decided early to dress and act like a male? Now I know it is not probable that George is really Georgina, but it is *possible*. (Note: you will hear the sentence "it is possible" several times in *12 Angry Men*, the first movie to be considered here!)

To say it again, Hume argues that any sentence must be either analytic or synthetic. If he is correct, why does skepticism follow? Because, though analytic sentences are true, they do not convey information about the world and thus are empty; and, though synthetic sentences purport to convey information about the world, they are possibly false. Any sentence is either analytic and empty or it is synthetic and possibly false.

Argument No. 3: "The analysis of the idea of causality"

As we saw in Argument No. 1, for Hume, "All ideas are copies of impressions." What happens if we *think* we have an idea but there is no corresponding impression? Our thought is incorrect? No. We don't have an idea. Where there is no content, there is no idea. Throw out the so-called idea. It is nonsense. (Think of it: non-sense. It is not obtained from sensory impressions. It is nonsense, ridiculous.)

In his epistemological works, Hume seeks the source of various ideas such as "free will," "God," and "miracles." An idea that Hume thinks is ever present in all judgments about the way the world is, is the idea of "causality." As he put it: "All reasonings concerning matter of fact seem to be founded on the relation of *Cause and Effect*."[6] He wants to know what impressions are the source of our idea of a cause and effect relation. The results of his investigations are stunning and, once again, lead those who accept his train of thought to see that skepticism follows.

Central to Hume's analysis is his famous "billiard ball example." We think we know that one billiard ball "A" strikes another billiard ball "B," and that motion is imparted from A to B. From what impressions do we obtain our idea of ball A causing ball B to move? Well, try it yourself. Roll one ball towards another and carefully pay attention to the impressions you receive. I have asked students to describe exactly what they see when I roll one ball at another. Invariably they say, "I saw the first ball moving, I saw it hit the second ball, and I saw the second ball moving." I suspect you, the reader, would respond the same way. *But you would be wrong!* You do not see ball A hitting ball B. You *believe* it hits B! Look again. You see one event — ball A moving closer and closer to ball B — and then another event — ball B moving. And that is all! Perhaps A did not hit B! Perhaps a magnet in A repelled B. Perhaps someone with a remote control caused B to move when A got close. The important point, again, is that you did not have an impression of A hitting B. We believe A hit B because the motion of B followed the motion of A. We do not know that the event of B moving is necessarily connected to the event of A moving. Every case in which we believe one event causes another event is open to the same type of analysis as that found in the "billiard ball example." We are possibly mistaken any time we make judgments about cause and effect. All we saw was one event followed by another event! We cannot know that any particular event is the cause of some other event. And that implies skepticism.

Henry Fonda (left) and Lee J. Cobb (right) head an all-star cast in *12 Angry Men* (1957).

After you watch each of the first four movies (*12 Angry Men*, *The Return of Martin Guerre*, *House of Games*, and *Rashomon*), think about the three Humean arguments outlined. The four movies are very different from one another. Still, utilizing Hume's arguments in analyzing those movies will provide much to think about.

Movie 1: *12 Angry Men*

Director: Sidney Lumet; 1 hour, 36 minutes; 1957
Watch the movie.

Questions to ponder:

1. The phrase "reasonable doubt" plays a crucial role in 12 Angry Men. How would you define "reasonable doubt?"
2. Do you think the accused youth is guilty? How would you have

voted before Davis (Henry Fonda) stood alone? How would you have voted by the end of the movie?

3. Of course, *12 Angry Men* is fictional, but you may be surprised by this: I still think the kid is guilty. The knife falls through his pants. Ha! Would *anyone* be judged guilty if Davis were on the jury? Do you think Davis got a murderer off the hook?

4. List the "facts" about the case that were shown to involve synthetic judgments, i.e., sentences that are possibly false. (Davis even says, "It's possible!" when fellow jurors complain of an improbable conjecture.)

5. Many people do not give an "old" black and white movie a chance. Do you think the drama of the film is lessened because it is in black and white? Is it lessened because most of the action takes place in one room? Most people who are told that *12 Angry Men* contains little action, and that the bulk of the movie takes place in two rooms, would probably be very surprised by how intense and interesting *12 Angry Men* is.

6. Juror number three (Lee J. Cobb) is the last juror to vote "not guilty." Were you convinced by his switch, which seems to occur only when he becomes aware of his own bitterness against all young men because of his disappointment in his own son?

NOTE: Those who see all the movies covered in this book will be exposed to two other films that utilize limited sets. (I won't disclose the titles now.) Another powerful movie that features only one setting is *Tape* (2001).

Movie 2: *The Return of Martin Guerre*

Director: Daniel Vigne; 2 hours, 3 minutes; 1982

The Return of Martin Guerre would make a great fictional story. Here, however, is one of those cases in which fact is as amazing as fiction. Natalie Zemon Davis, the author of an historical account of the Martin Guerre story, served as a consultant for the movie.[7] The primary source material for Davis' work is the detailed report of Jean de Coras, one of the medieval judges who was involved in the trials depicted in the film.

Watch the movie.

Questions to ponder:

1. Did Bertrande (Nathalie Baye) know that the returning "Martin" (Gerard Depardieu) was an imposter? Wouldn't a woman know inti-

Gerard Depardieu and Nathalie Baye in *The Return of Martin Guerre* (1982).

mate details about her husband and be able to recognize him even after eight years?

2. As portrayed in the movie, the imposter (whose real name was Arnaud du Tilh) and Bertrande truly loved one another. Should du Tilh have been executed? He was an adulterer, and, as the historian Natalie Zemon Davis puts it, his crime "involved stealing a heritage, which could be compared to a woman's misrepresenting her illegitimate child to her husband as his own so that the child could inherit."[8]

3. Should the real Martin Guerre be charged for deserting Bertrande? According to Davis, the court decided "his departure could be attributed to 'the heat and levity of youth,' which was then boiling up in him." The court ruled that he had been punished enough due to "what had happened to his leg, to his goods, and to his wife."[9] Was the punishment enough for what he did?

Comments on *Sommersby*, a remake of *The Return of Martin Guerre*:

A substitute for *The Return of Martin Guerre* would be *Sommersby* (1993), starring Richard Gere and Jodie Foster. *Sommersby*, an American remake of *The Return of Martin Guerre*, is fairly well done, but such retellings are seldom as good as the original. This remake is set during the American Civil War. Unlike the French original, it fails to become a great movie. David Edelstein, in an article entitled "Remade in America: A Label to Avoid," put it this way:

> The problem with translations goes deeper than the lack of originality … to what one might term the DNA of cinema. In Richard Linklater's recent animated feature, *Waking Life*, a professor (Caveh Zahedi) paraphrases the essential doctrine of the French theorist Andre Bazin: that film can capture "*that* guy in *that* moment in *that* space." Bazin called it "the holy moment" and argued that when you succeed in getting "ontological reality" on film, you have a permanent record of the "everlasting face of God."
>
> God is palpably absent from, say, the American version of *The Vanishing*, probably the most maladroit of all Hollywood adaptations. A filmmaker laboring to duplicate something he or someone else has already done doesn't have a prayer of discovering "the holy moment." He's too busy asking: "Uh, how did it go this last time? Where was the light? Was the guy standing here or there?" The spark, the fever of creation, inevitably dies: the action feels predetermined, as if it had already happened a long time ago in a galaxy far, far away.

Edelstein goes on to refer specifically to *Sommersby* and its "gingerly" treatment of "sex outside marriage."

> The French Martin is cold and sexually dysfunctional, so when a warm and hunky imposter (Gerard Depardieu) arrives, it's enough that he works hard and shows his predecessor's love-starved wife (Nathalie Baye) a good time in the sack. In *Sommersby* (1993) the real husband isn't just a creep but a racist, wife-beating murderer—and he's dead to boot, so there's really no moral downside when the wife (Jodie Foster) jumps into bed with the pretender (Richard Gere). Together they create a racial, economic and sexual utopia…. *Sommersby* weaves a rich tapestry, but the simple and mysterious erotic heartbeat of *The Return of Martin Guerre* (1982) is here not even a murmur.[10]

Still, you might be interested in reviewing *Sommersby* just to see how it handles the imposter angle.

The movie *The Vanishing* mentioned in the above quote is one of the most frightening films ever made. Watch the original. But again, you may want to check out the remake.

Joseph Mantegna in David Mamet's *House of Games* (1987).

By the bye, if you enjoyed Gerard Depardieu in *Martin Guerre*, look for his other masterpieces. For example, see *Jean de Florette* (1986). *Jean de Florette* is not a complete movie; the plot continues in *Manon of the Spring* (1986). However, Depardieu does not appear in *Manon*. Another Depardieu masterpiece is *Cyrano de Bergerac* (1990).

Movie 3: *House of Games*

Director: David Mamet; 1 hour, 41 minutes; 1987

There is something about David Mamet's *House of Games* that turns off some viewers. I'll prepare you for that element of the film, and that knowledge may heighten your appreciation and enjoyment of the movie. For Mamet, it is the director who counts in the making of a movie, and because "most actors are, unfortunately, not good actors," an actor should "do his simple physical actions as simply as possible."[11] In *House of Games* the actors speak in a monotone. Does it work? Yes. Would I want all movies to contain actors merely speaking in a monotone? No, of course not.

Watch the movie.

Questions to ponder:

1. Remember that Hume held that people are incorrect when they say they see one billiard ball strike another billiard ball. Note how similar is the lesson Dr. Ford (Lindsay Crouse) learns when she is corrected after saying, "I saw you put the $20 bill in the envelope." She does *not* see the bill being placed in the envelope. Every step in the chain of events set off by Mike (Joe Mantegna) and his fellow con artists involves both Dr. Ford's and the viewer's assumption that they saw more than they indeed saw. That's why Dr. Ford is so shocked when she realizes she has been conned by Mike — a person she believed cared for her. Give other examples from the film that verify Hume's point.

2. In an important sense it can be said that Mike does not deceive Maggie Ford. When she asks to accompany him to see how the con game works, Mike says, "You want to see how a true bad man plies his trade?" Well, he shows her. However, there is an excellent chance that Mike conned *you* the viewer! As thoroughly as possible, answer the following question before reading on: What happened in the airport near the end of the movie? I'll bet you give the wrong answer — as you'll see when you turn to the next question.

Akira Kurosawa's *Rashomon* (1950) starring Machiko Kyo (left) and Toshiro Mifune (right).

3. If in your answer to the above question you say, "Maggie killed Mike," then think again. A wonderful con has been pulled on you! Mike is not dead! What Mike is doing is called in the con game "erasing the mark." As long as Maggie (the mark) is angry at being conned, she is a threat to the con artist. If Mike can make her satisfied with her situation, he has "erased the mark." At the end of the film, Maggie is happy. (Notice that for the first time she wears colorful clothing.) Though she doesn't know it, Mike and his friends are spending her money. Now figure out why the statement "Maggie killed Mike" is false. What clues in the movie prove it false? Listed below are some of the clues. Do not look at those sentences until you have *really* tried to figure out what happened in the movie.

Some clues:

(1) The gun Maggie used to "kill" Mike was the gun given her by Billy Hahn (Steven Goldstein), who was clearly part of Mike's gang of con men.

(2) Another "killing" was already shown to be fake — the killing of the policeman in the hotel. That policeman was one of the con men.

(3) The car Jimmie drove after his last meeting with Maggie in her office was the same car the con men supposedly ditched after fleeing the hotel. Jimmie parked it close enough to Maggie's office so she would see it.

Movie 4: *Rashomon*

Director: Akira Kurosawa; 1 hour, 28 minutes; 1950
Watch the movie.

Questions to ponder:

1. In his book *Something Like an Autobiography*, Kurosawa says about *Rashomon*:

> Human beings are unable to be honest with themselves. They cannot talk about themselves without embellishing. This script portrays such human beings — the kind who cannot survive without lies to make them feel they are better people than they really are.... Egoism is a sin the human being carries with him from birth; it is the most difficult to redeem.... You say you can't understand the script at all, but that is because the human heart itself is impossible to understand.

> If you focus on the impossibility of truly understanding human psychology and read the script one more time, I think you will grasp the point of it![12]

It may be impossible to tell, but what do you think really happens in the grove? What parts of the various testimonies are lies? What parts were true? Is there any evidence that isn't brought forward that could have led to a clearer picture of what happened? For example, wouldn't an investigator of the fatal wound that killed the husband (Masayuki Mori) have known whether a dagger was used (the woodsman [Takashi Shimura] would be the murderer) or a sword (depending on the way the sword entered the body might determine if the death was a suicide or occurred at the hands of the bandit [Toshiro Mifune])?

Kurosawa is without a doubt one of the greatest directors of all time. If you enjoyed *Rashomon*, try the following Kurosawa movies:

Ikiru (1952)
The Seven Samurai (1954)
Throne of Blood (1957): Kurosawa's rendition of *Macbeth*
Yojimbo (1961)
High and Low (1963): This is a murder mystery based on a work by Ed McBain, the American best-selling author.
Red Beard (1965)
Dersu Uzala (1975)
Kagemusha (1980)
Ran (1985): Kurosawa's interpretation of *King Lear*
Akira Kurosawa's Dreams (1990)
Rhapsody in August (1991)
Madadayo (1993)

In addition, *Kurosawa: A Documentary on the Acclaimed Director* (2000) covers his entire life and work. It is well edited and very informative. A beautifully produced book is *The Films of Akira Kurosawa*, 3rd edition, by Donald Richie (Berkeley: University of California Press, 1996).

In most of the early films listed above, you will find Toshiro Mifune playing the lead roles. He is the bandit in *Rashomon*. Though he often seems to overact, most viewers will learn to appreciate his acting style.

ADDITIONAL RECOMMENDATIONS FOR THE TOPIC
"DID YOU EVER THINK YOU KNEW SOMETHING, BUT DIDN'T?"

The Crying Game (1992). Warning: Violence, Nudity. Several haunting scenes, one so unexpected it will stay with you forever. Like *Full Metal Jacket* (Movie 38), *The Crying Game* is made up of two acts. Stephen Rea plays Fergus, and is the lead character in both acts. Forrest Whitaker gives an unforgettable performance in the first act as a British soldier captured by the IRA.

M (1931). People who loved *Silence of the Lambs* should give *M* a chance. Peter Lorre stars and shows why he was one of the big stars of yesteryear. Fritz Lang, the innovative filmmaker who gave us *Metropolis* (1927), directed.

A Simple Plan (1998). Great question: What would *you* do if you found what the characters in the film find?

Miller's Crossing (1990). One of the Coen Brothers' best films. Gabriel Byrne is excellent. Compare his role here with that in *The Usual Suspects* (Movie 72). *Miller's Crossing* is a gangster movie. As the plot unfolds, it is difficult to tell who can be trusted. In my view, *Barton Fink* (1991) and *Fargo* (1996) join *Miller's Crossing* as the Coen Brothers' best works.

2

The Greatest Happiness Principle

The major tenet of philosophers known as utilitarians is called "the principle of utility" or "the greatest happiness principle." John Stuart Mill (1806–1873), the most famous utilitarian, wrote:

> The creed which accepts as the foundation of morals "Utility" or the "greatest happiness principle" holds that actions are right in proportion as they tend to promote happiness; wrong as they tend to produce the reverse of happiness.[1]

It is important to note that the happiness promoted is not just one's own happiness. Rather, utilitarians stress the moral value of bringing the greatest amount of happiness to the greatest number of people. The happiness of anyone who will be affected by one's moral decision should be considered — including the happiness of the decision maker.

Jeremy Bentham (1748–1832), the founder of Utilitarianism, presented a list of criteria that must be addressed before a final judgment can be made about what decision would tend to bring about the greatest amount of happiness. That list is now called the "pleasure/pain calculus." Here, in Bentham's words, is the calculus:

> To a *number* of persons, with reference to each of whom the value of a pleasure or a pain is considered, it will be greater or less, according to seven circumstances ... viz.
>
> 1. Its intensity.
> 2. Its duration.
> 3. Its certainty or uncertainty.
> 4. Its propinquity or remoteness.
> 5. Its fecundity.
> 6. Its purity.

And one other; to wit:

    7. Its extent: that is, the number of persons to whom it extends...[2]

In other words, the intensity of the pleasures and pains that arise as a result of a decision should be considered, as well as how long they endure, how certain or uncertain it is that they will arise again, whether they will arise in the near or far future, whether they will be "followed by sensations of the same kind" (fecundity) and what "chance it has of *not* being followed by sensations of the opposite kind: that is, pain if it be pleasure: pleasure, if it be pain" (purity).[3]

The standard interpretation of Bentham's calculus is that all the questions it requires one to ask are questions dealing with *quantitative* matters. ("How many people will experience pleasure?" "How intense are the pleasures and pains that will arise?") Mill, whose father was a close friend of Bentham, held that *qualitative* issues must also be addressed by persons making a moral decision. What is the quality of the pleasure that a decision will tend to bring about? Humans are capable of higher and lower pleasures. As Mill says, "A beast's pleasures do not satisfy a human being's conceptions of happiness."[4] Mill not only distinguishes humans from beasts (lower animals), but also makes a distinction between humans who possess "higher faculties" and those who possess "lower faculties." The latter are satisfied with lowly pleasures that would satisfy beasts.

A person with higher faculties, Mill says, "requires more to make him happy," and is "capable probably of more acute suffering."[5] From this distinction, between those who have higher faculties and those who lack those faculties, Mill derives one of his most famous sayings: "It is better to be a human being dissatisfied than a pig satisfied. And, if the fool, or the pig, are of a different opinion, it is because they only know their own side of the question. The other party to the comparison knows both sides."[6]

The end of the above quote provides an answer to an objection often leveled against Mill. The critic asks, "Who is to judge what is a higher vs. a lower pleasure?" Mill's answer is that the best judge is the person with the broadest experience. "Of two pleasures, if there be one to which all or almost all who have experience of both give a decided preference ... that is the more desirable pleasure."[7]

An illustration of Mill's concept of a "good judge of pleasure" will help. I give it to many of my students because most undergraduates are "moral relativists." They believe that all moral judgments are mere opinions dependent on one's cultural conditioning. A very common question they ask is, "Who knows what's right or wrong, good or bad?" The illustration I give is taken from personal experience: I have always loved rock and roll. I remember the first time I heard Little Richard's "Lucille." It was at a town fair. All around me people grumbled about "Lucille," calling it "noise" and "jungle music." I was enthralled by the sound, its originality and its drive. I remember the day Buddy Holly died. I was crushed. Elvis, the King! The Beatles, The Clash, AC/DC. (I hear some of you groan.) I loved them all. When I was young I used to make judgments about classical music. "Man, how dull. Constipated music. Hard to play — but give me the beat of rock! Rock rocks!" Then one summer I was in Aspen, Colorado. Friends were going to the "Aspen Music Tent" to hear some boring group called the "Juilliard String Quartet." I had nothing better to do, so I went along. My friends and I sat outside the music tent, which was both legal and free. The Quartet started to play. The sky was a wonderful blue. Gliders soared in the mountain fresh air. Looking north I could see the beautiful peaks of the Maroon Bells, snow-topped even in July.... And then — *I heard the music.* I heard it and it was *wonderful!* I now have a great collection of classical music. I've attended the Metropolitan Opera. I sat on the stage seven feet from Evgeny Kissin during one of his concerts. Who is the better judge of classical music — me, before I experienced its pleasures and only appreciated rock and roll? Or me, after I appreciated *both* forms of music? The answer is clear! My students are (sometimes) wrong when they assert there are never better and worse judges of matters dealing with values.

My illustration, however, has to do with aesthetic taste. There are additional problems with the position that some people are better judges of moral decisions than others. Who is a good judge of such matters? I will lead to at least a partial answer to those questions by exploring a fictional scenario. (Bear with me — this scenario will be *strange*.) Suppose there is a man named Amos who has learned from some obscure mystical work how to perform a sexual trick that gives its recipient(s) the most intense orgasm possible. Not only that, anyone who experiences the Amos-caused orgasm can, in the future, attain orgasm merely by remembering the original one. Even ten years after the original experience, the orgasm can be recaptured. Amos isn't thrilled about sharing his trick and usually turns down requests to share it. A friend — without asking Amos first — announced to fifty acquaintances from all over the United States that there would be an orgy on a certain date. Amos would share his trick at the orgy. The fifty pilgrims gather in Amos' town. They can only stay for one hour and then must leave, never to return. This is their only chance to experience Amos' sexual trick. Now, the friend approaches Amos and tells him what he has done and asks Amos if he would please come to share his trick with his fifty visitors. Amos wants to say no, and is angry at his friend for not asking his permission first, but Amos is a good guy and tells his friend to go inform the fifty people he will be there in about ten minutes. The friend goes to inform the pilgrims. Amos slowly makes his way towards the gathering. However, before he gets there he witnesses a hit-and-run accident. A car hits a pedestrian and speeds off. Amos runs to aid the pedestrian. It is clear that the injuries are so severe that the pedestrian must get to a hospital immediately. If you were a utilitarian, what would you say Amos should do? Help the pedestrian or go to the orgy? If he helps the pedestrian, the fifty pilgrims will not experience intense pleasure during the orgy and for years afterwards by merely remembering Amos' trick. If he tries to help the pedestrian, fifty extremely disappointed people will disperse and return to their homes in other parts of the United States. One klutzy pedestrian versus fifty people?

It might appear that the utilitarians would choose the orgy because of the number of recipients of pleasure and the enduring pleasure they can recapture for years into the future. But that appearance is incorrect. First of all, the fifty-to-one ratio is misleading. The injured person has relatives and friends. Not only that, but the depth of suffering which would arise as the injured person watches Amos walk away must be considered. And what about the depth of suffering in society if it was learned that a person chose to go to an orgy rather than help someone in great need? And would Amos be a happier person if he went to the orgy or if he helped the injured person? Only a person who is satisfied with "pigpen pleasures" would choose the orgy over helping someone live. Such a person is actually miserable — but would not realize it unless he or she underwent a major character change and learned to experience the personal satisfaction of helping someone in need.

Movie 5: *Abandon Ship*

Director: Richard Sale; 1 hour, 37 minutes; 1956

The acting in *Abandon Ship* is outdated, and the special effects are far from special. However, the movie captures the difficult decisions faced by persons who accept the ethical philosophy called Utilitarianism.

Watch the movie.

Comments about the movie:

It sure seems that Sam (Orlando Martins) spent too much time in the water compared to other characters.

Anyway, a traditional nickname for Utilitarianism is "lifeboat ethics," and thus *Abandon Ship* is a wonderful presentation of the dilemmas faced by anyone such as Alec (Tyrone Power) who must try to save as many of a group as possible or risk losing every member of the group. Kelly (Lloyd Nolan) is a true utilitarian when he says, "Ya gotta evict some of the tenants," and, "I thought ya had guts enough to save half of them instead of losing them all."

Tyrone Power stars in *Abandon Ship* (1956).

An interesting scene occurs when a passenger suggests that everyone introduce themselves and give information about themselves. Kelly says to Alec, "Don't get to know them too well." Why? Because it may become too difficult to "evict" somebody.

However, each character does start to tell about himself or herself. One is a nuclear physicist, one an opera singer, and so forth. What people do in their lives often makes a major difference to utilitarians. However, in *Abandon Ship* such information is insignificant. The ones chosen to survive must be the "fittest." Alec stresses the "survival of the fittest" because only the fit will be able to help row the boat the great distance to safety. (I find one possible inconsistency here: Alec never suggests that the Kilgore's young son be thrown overboard.)

In some of my classes I set up the scenario in which a plane will crash if a person is not "evicted." I allow students to place people on the airplane. As it turns out, the airplane has a passenger list that includes people such as Adolf Hitler, Ted Bundy, Mother Theresa, a pregnant woman, the college's football coach, the current President of the United States, and the students' Philosophy professor. Of course, most students throw out Hitler. However — and I'm not making this up — there invariably will be a number of students who, in all seriousness, choose the President or the football coach over Hitler to discard. What can one say to such students?

Questions to ponder:

1. Do you agree with the character who says, "The whole point of civilization is for the strong to protect the weak?" Does *Abandon Ship* provide an exception to that rule?

2. Is Alec a murderer? Should he have been brought to trial? If you were a member of the jury, how would you have voted: Guilty or Not Guilty?

3. After the storm, when the passengers realize they will be safe, they wholeheartedly praise Alec for his courageous decisions. Yet by the end of the movie they literally and symbolically turn their backs on him. Why?

4. Since Alec is the strongest leader, should he have included himself as one who would "go over the side like anyone else" if the situation called for it? Does the fact that he is sincere in his willingness to sacrifice

his own life for the good of the greatest number add to the merit of his decisions?

An additional recommendation:

If you enjoyed *Abandon Ship*, try Alfred Hitchcock's 1944 almost forgotten masterpiece *Lifeboat*. You will be stunned by the similarities between the two films, but will also enjoy the differences. Tallulah Bankhead is excellent in *Lifeboat*. A kiss between Tallulah and William Bendix is a moment no one should miss. Both films allot only one black person per lifeboat. The black actor in *Lifeboat* is Canada Lee, an actor possessing stunning charisma. The big question to be answered after viewing *Lifeboat*: "Should the German have been thrown out of the boat?"

Movie 6: *The Field*

Director: Jim Sheridan; 1 hour, 53 minutes; 1990

You may have some difficulty understanding the Irish accents in *The Field*, but bear with the movie. Richard Harris gives an unforgettable performance as "Bull McCabe." For his role, Harris received a Best Actor Oscar nomination.

Watch the movie.

Questions to ponder:

1. Would the villagers in *The Field* be better off if Bull McCabe had his way, or if the "Yank" (Tom Berenger) had his? Which of the two would bring the greatest amount of happiness to the area? Are you considering the *quality* of the happiness when you provide your answer?

2. Does the Yank really care about the area or only about the profit to be gained by his enterprises?

3. Is the field *just* a field? Is it more? What more?

4. Given the facts that Bull dedicated his life to the field, his mother died there, and his father entrusted the

Richard Harris as Bull McCabe in *The Field* (1990).

field to him, does Bull have a greater right to the field than the Yank who has the legal right? If he does, is his attempt to drive the Yank away justified?

5. Was Bull a good man? A bully?

3

Doing One's Duty

Immanuel Kant (1724–1804) is generally considered one of the greatest philosophers in the Western tradition. In his major works he regularly asks questions of the form, "What is necessary for the possibility of X?" In his *Critique of Pure Reason* and *Prolegomena to One's Future Metaphysics*, X = knowledge. In the *Critique of Practical Reason* and *Foundations of the Metaphysics of Morals*, X = morality. A central concept in his answers to the question, "What is necessary for the possibility of morality?" is the idea of "duty."

Here, in outline, are three major points from Kant's ethical theory:

I. When making a moral decision, a person with good will will not consider possible consequences of the decision. Kant would be unalterably opposed to Utilitarianism, which stresses that a moral decision is good if it tends to bring about the greatest amount of happiness to the greatest number of people. As Kant puts it, "the moral worth of an action does not lie in the effect which is expected from it..."[1] A person can be good even if desired effects do not arise. Plus, an ethical theory based on human judgment of future events has, according to Kant, a very shaky foundation. Humans are not God and do not know the future.

II. A decision has moral worth if, and only if, it is made out of duty to a moral law. Decisions made out of self-interest or out of "inclination" are not done out of duty, and anyone motivated by either self-interest or inclination is not acting morally.

III. Kant labels the moral law that any rational person can discover as "the Categorical Imperative." This moral law is similar to the Golden Rule. Kant's most famous formulation of the Categorical Imperative is: "Act only according to that maxim by which you can at the same time will that it should become a universal law."[2]

Kant presents a series of examples to show how the Categorical Imperative should be the guide for those people making moral decisions. Here are two of his examples:

> [A] man finds himself forced by need to borrow money. He well knows that he will not be able to repay it, but he also sees that nothing will be loaned him if he does not firmly promise to repay it at a certain time. He desires to make such a promise, but he has enough conscience to ask himself whether it is not improper and opposed to duty to relieve his distress in such a way. Now, assuming he does decide to do so, the maxim of his action would be as follows: When I believe myself to be in need of money, I will borrow money and promise to repay it, although I know I shall never do so. Now this principle of self-love or of his own benefit may very well be compatible with his whole future welfare, but the question is whether it is right. He changes the pretension of self-love into a universal law and then puts the question: How would it be if my maxim became a universal law? He immediately sees that it could never hold as a universal law of nature and be consistent with itself; rather it must necessarily contradict itself. For the universality of a law which says that anyone who believes himself to be in need could promise what he pleased with the intention of not fulfilling it would make the promise itself and the end to be accomplished by it impossible; no one would believe what was promised to him but would only laugh at any such assertion as vain pretense.[3]

A human being who borrows money and promises to pay it back, even though he knows he will not be able to do so, is acting out of "self-love" or self-interest. If everyone promised to repay X with "the intention of not fulfilling it," the practice of promising would cease to exist. No one would believe any promises. Thus, for Kant, an intention not to fulfill a promise breaks the moral rule called "the Categorical Imperative" and should be called an "immoral intention."

The next example stresses that it is immoral to fail to develop our natural talents:

> Another man finds in himself a talent which could, by means of some cultivation, make him in many respects a useful man. But he finds himself in comfortable circumstances and prefers indulgence in pleasure to troubling himself with broadening and improving his fortunate natural gifts. Now, however, let him ask whether his maxim of neglecting his gifts, besides agreeing with his propensity to idle amusement, agrees also with what is called duty. He sees that a system of nature could indeed exist in accordance with such a law, even though man (like the

inhabitants of the South Sea Islands) should let his talents rust and resolve to devote his life merely to idleness, indulgence, and propagation — in a word, to pleasure. But he cannot possibly will that this should become a universal law of nature or that it should be implanted in us by a natural instinct. For, as a rational being, he necessarily wills that all his faculties should be developed, inasmuch as they are given to him for all sorts of possible purposes.[4]

In the above example, Kant argues that it is everyone's duty to develop their talents. Note that in the example, Kant breaks his own Categorical Imperative by making a prejudiced statement about a whole class of humans with whom he had no contact: South Sea Islanders. He judges that all such people live in idleness, are interested only in material goods, and engage in lots of sexual activity.

The two movies you will watch will center on characters who choose to do their duty.

Movie 7: *High Noon*

Director: Fred Zinnemann; 1 hour, 25 minutes; 1952
Watch the movie.

Questions to ponder:

1. The theme song at the beginning of the movie mentions being "torn between love and duty." Should Kane (Gary Cooper) have chosen love or duty? Why? What should Amy (Grace Kelly) have chosen? (She was a Quaker, and her faith held it was her duty to oppose violence.) Is either Kane or Amy following Kant's Categorical Imperative?

2. As noon approaches, men of the town are shown at the church and at the saloon. They look ashamed that they are not helping Kane. Did Kane have a good reason *not* to stay because the townspeople failed to support him? Does his duty to stay cease if he has no support from the people he is trying to protect?

Movie 8: *The Road Home*

Director: Zhang Yimou; 1 hour, 29 minutes; 2000
Watch the movie.

Gary Cooper in *High Noon* (1952).

Ziyi Zhang in *The Road Home* (2000).

Questions to ponder:

1. Is the mother (Zhao Yuelin) just a bull-headed old woman who should be satisfied having a tractor bring the body of her husband home? Given the fact that she is weak, and weaving is very hard work, isn't her son (Sun Honglei) correct that they should purchase a coffin cover? Can one understand the bringing-home-on-a-tractor and buying-the-cloth ideas without bringing the concept of

duty into the picture? After all, since the father taught in the town for 40 years and died as a result of getting caught in a storm while trying to raise money for the school, isn't it the case that, "the town has a duty to give him something back"?

2. Does the son have a duty to fulfill his *mother's* wishes? Why do you think he taught a lesson in the schoolhouse?

4

Anxiety and Inauthenticity

The philosophical movement called "Existentialism" is one of the most influential forces behind a great deal of the art, literature, music, and film of the 20th century.

It is difficult to define "Existentialism," in part because there are two groups of Existentialists — those who are "religious" and those who are atheistic. The former includes Soren Kierkegaard (1813–1855), whose works constitute the beginning of Religious Existentialism. Friedrich Nietzsche (1844–1900) is known as the intellectual stimulus for Atheistic Existentialism. Other existentialists include:

Religious Existentialists	*Atheistic Existentialists*
Paul Tillich	Jean-Paul Sartre
Martin Buber	Simone DeBeauvoir
Karl Jaspers	Albert Camus
Miguel de Unamuno	
Martin Heidegger[1]	

In their writings, all existentialists — whether religious or atheistic — regularly cover certain themes that jointly constitute the essence of Existentialism. These existential themes include:

1. A stress on the worth of the human individual, and the importance of the individual accepting responsibility for his or her actions. Most existentialists hold that the individual is a free agent.

2. A stress on this world and a harsh attitude towards what Nietzsche calls "other-worldly thought," thought that projects a realm that is better than the earthly realm. (Plato's world of Forms, and the Christian heaven, are "other worlds.")

3. The view that all humans are filled with "angst." Angst is deep-

32

seated anxiety present during every waking moment. Some existentialists link angst with an awareness that one's death is on the horizon. (For an exploration of this idea, see Movie 30: *Fearless.*) Others link angst with the uncertainty about what decisions to make on important matters.

4. "The absurdity of existence." Though existentialists are "this-worldly," they all see the universe and human life as filled with the irrational. So much of life is meaningless, empty.

5. The difficulty communicating with other people. (Some religious existentialists would also stress the difficulty of communicating with God. Buber, for example, held that at certain times, as during the Holocaust, there seems to be an "eclipse" of God.)

6. The stress on the value of solitude and a distrust of "crowds." Kierkegaard is noted for his statement, "The crowd is untruth," and Nietzsche refers to groups of humans as "herds."

7. The importance of "existential rebellion." Such rebellion has to do with asserting one's own unique being against those who attempt to mold others in their own image. In her classic work *The Second Sex,* Simone de Beauvoir promoted feminist rebellion against a male-dominated culture. Camus' great work *The Rebel* also centers on the theme of existential rebellion.

I have chosen three movies that contain existential themes: *Hannah and Her Sisters, My Dinner with Andre* and *About Schmidt.*

Movie 9: *Hannah and Her Sisters*

Director: Woody Allen; 1 hour, 47 minutes; 1986

Viewers either love Woody Allen movies or hate them. My contention is that most people who hate them have never really given them a chance. Give *Hannah and Her Sisters* a chance; you may be surprised! Watch the movie.

Questions to ponder:

1. Can you spot the following existential themes in the movie?
   a. The difficulty communicating with others
   b. The absurdity of the universe
   c. Angst
   d. "This-worldliness"

Mia Farrow (left) as Hannah, and Barbara Hershey (center) and Diane Wiest as her sisters, in Woody Allen's *Hannah and Her Sisters* (1986).

2. Frederick (Max Von Sydow) possesses several characteristics of the existentialist. However, he comes across as inauthentic. Why?

3. A crucial scene, filled with existential meaning, is that in which Mickey (Woody Allen) enters a theater and watches a Marx Brothers movie. What is the relevance of that scene?

Comment:

Did you answer Question 3 above with any confidence? Here's my answer. In watching the absurd antics of the Marx Brothers, Mickey receives what I would call "existential enlightenment." From merely being a pessimist, filled with deep-seated angst at his own impending death, Mickey accepts the absurdity of the universe and affirms this life. At the conclusion of his famous retelling of "The Myth of Sisyphus," Albert Camus announces, "One must imagine Sisyphus happy." Sisyphus, condemned by the gods to eternally roll a rock up a mountain just to have it roll back down, accepts his absurd life. In *The Stranger*, Camus has Meursault affirming this life even as he walks to his own execution. In his later works, Martin Heidegger stresses that one's life can serve as a "clearing of Being." For the most part, humans walk through life like they are lost in a dark forest without much hope of finding a way out. Suddenly, however, they may come to a clearing and can — at least temporarily — achieve an authentic relation with Being. Examples of things that might provide such a clearing, according to Heidegger, are paintings by Van Gogh and poems by Holderlin. In *Hannah and Her Sisters* Mickey achieves such a clearing through the Marx Brothers movie.

If you wish to check out other Woody Allen films, here is a list of some of his best work:

Take the Money and Run (1969)
Bananas (1971)
Play It Again, Sam (1972)
Everything You Always Wanted to Know About Sex (1972)
Sleeper (1973)
Annie Hall (1977)
Manhattan (1979)
Zelig (1983)
Broadway Danny Rose (1984)
Radio Days (1987)
Crimes and Misdemeanors (1989)
Husbands and Wives (1992)
Mighty Aphrodite (1995)
Everyone Says I Love You (1996)
Deconstructing Harry (1997)
Sweet and Lowdown (1999)

In addition, see *Wild Man Blues* (1997), a documentary covering a European concert tour undertaken by Woody Allen and his jazz band. Barbara Kopple directed. Her documentary about striking Kentucky coal miners, *Harlan County, USA* (1976), won an Oscar for Best Documentary.

Movie 10: *My Dinner with Andre*

Director: Louis Malle; 1 hour, 50 minutes; 1981
If you let yourself get into the flow of it, you will see that *My Dinner*

Wally (Wallace Shawn) listens intently during his dinner with Andre (Andre Gregory). Andre can be seen in the mirror.

with Andre is a very powerful movie. Be forewarned: the "flow" I just mentioned is not like any other you have experienced in a movie. This flow is the flow of a dinner conversation between Andre (Andre Gregory) and Wally (Wallace Shawn)—an almost-two-hour-long discussion. One of my students said it might work as a play, but "a movie should *move!*" That student missed whatever it was that led many critics to rave about the film and whatever it is that astonishes me and *moves* me to tears every time I view it. However, the last two times I viewed it, I thought the first third of the conversation was a little weird and draggy, but was necessary for what would come later.

All of the existential themes I mentioned in my introduction to this chapter have a prominent place in *My Dinner with Andre*. So sit back and relax! (but don't fall asleep). Let this dinner conversation move you. Let it elevate you.

Watch the movie.

Questions to ponder:

1. What existential themes did you spot in the dinner conversation?

2. The published screenplay of *My Dinner with Andre* says of the waiter (Jean Lenauer): "His face shows that he has seen and experienced the suffering of the world."[2] Did you see that?

3. Is Andre crazy? When I saw the movie the first time, I was with a friend. I asked my friend what he thought would be the course of Andre's life after the meeting with Wally. My friend said: "He committed suicide." I disagree. I see Andre as what existentialists call the "absurd hero" — one who is filled with angst but who continues to struggle to create meaning in a meaningless, absurd world. Do you tend to agree with me — or my friend?

4. Andre seems to think humanity has entered a new Dark Age where we are all "feeling nothing, thinking nothing," where we are all bored and have affairs or watch TV in order to cover up our lifeless lives. Do you agree with Andre? Wally doesn't agree. He says: "I just don't know how anybody could enjoy anything more than I enjoy reading Charlton Heston's autobiography.... I'm just so thrilled when I get up and see that coffee there. I just don't think I feel the need for anything more than all this. Whereas you seem to be saying it is inconceivable that anybody could be having a meaningful life today." Is Wally in the Dark Age I previously mentioned? Wally wants to be a successful playwright like Andre. Will he achieve that success if he does not heed Andre's advice? Will he be successful if he is satisfied reading Charlton Heston's autobiography?

Comments:

1. A number of times throughout the film Andre expresses his awareness of the absurdity of the universe and the accompanying feeling that normal activities lack meaning. An example appears early in the movie. Andre had been asked to teach a workshop in Poland. "But," reports

Andre, "I didn't want to come, because really, I had nothing left to teach. I had nothing left to say. I didn't know anything. I couldn't teach anymore…. I didn't know what to do." Later he says, "I feel my whole life has been a sham."

2. It seems to me that, in the forest in Poland, Andre achieves the Nietzschean balance of seriousness and playfulness. "Forty people who don't speak your language. Then all your moorings are gone…. In a way it's like going right back to childhood where a group of children simply enter a room, without toys, and they begin to play. Grownups were learning how to play again…. What I think I experienced was for the first time in my life to know what it means to be truly alive."

3. Andre understands much of what Wally says but is aware that in many ways Wally is missing life. Wally's unwillingness to give up his electric blanket is one clue that leads to the conclusion that Wally is living a shallow existence. Andre says about the blanket, "But Wally, don't you see that comfort can be dangerous?" Is it noteworthy that Andre understands the menu, but Wally doesn't have a clue?

4. Nietzsche warns about the danger of the advent of the "last man." The "last man" is not excited about anything. He "blinks" when faced with greatness.[3] In a similar vein, Andre thinks, "We are all bored … this boredom that we see in the world now may very well be a self-perpetuating unconscious form of brainwashing created by a totalitarian world government based on money." We've imprisoned ourselves, says Andre, and don't even realize we're in a prison. In a sense, we just "blink."

Movie 11: *About Schmidt*

Director: Alexander Payne; 2 hour, 5 minutes; 2003
Watch the movie.

Questions to ponder:

1. What is the significance of the fact that many scenes in the film include cows? For example, at the establishment where Warren's (Jack Nicholson) retirement party takes place, there are pictures of cows on the walls. Several times on his road trip Warren notices cows.

2. The inevitability of future events and the dread we feel about some of those events is captured in the opening scene as Warren watches

Jeannie (Hope Davis) marries Randall (Dermot Mulroney). Jack Nicholson (middle) as Schmidt, Hope's father, looks on in *About Schmidt* (2003).

the clock tick toward 5:00 P.M. His dreaded retirement is about to begin. He is clearly dismayed by the fact that his future years will not be as productive, nor as meaningful, as the years he put in working at the insurance company. At Warren's retirement party his friend Ray (Len Cariou) says, "All those gifts over there don't mean a God-damned thing. And this dinner doesn't mean a God-damned thing. And the Social Security and pension don't mean a God-damned thing. None of these superficialities mean a God-damned thing. What counts is that Warren devoted his life to something meaningful. To being productive. Working for a fine company. Raising a fine family. Having wonderful friendships. So, all you young people here — take a good look at a very rich man." But are the things listed as "meaningful" as meaningful as Ray thinks? Or are they as "superficial" as Social Security? After all, the "fine company" is now glad to be rid of Warren. His daughter (Hope Davis) is marrying brainless Randall (Dermot Mulroney). His wife, Helen (June Squibb), nags him, and Ray, his good friend, previously had an adulterous affair with Helen. Doesn't Warren's whole life give evidence of the absurdity of existence?

3. In a very funny scene, Warren looks at sleeping Helen and wonders, "Who is this person?" Have you ever had the experience that people you have known intimately are really strangers — that you don't know them? Have you ever felt that way about yourself? If you look at yourself in a mirror, does it seem a stranger is peering back at you? Do we ever really know ourselves or other people? When we think we have such knowledge are we lying to ourselves?

4. One scene disturbed me. It seems to be a gross commercial exploitation with nothing of import to move the film's plot along. It is the scene in which Warren leaves his house right before Helen dies. Warren goes to a famous ice cream franchise and orders an item. Did you see that scene as possessing artistic relevance? A friend thought that it just shows Warren doing something small that had meaning to him. I reacted to that scene as I did to one in a recent version of *Hamlet* starring Ethan Hawke. In that film, the ghost of Hamlet's father disappears into a huge soda machine on which appears the logo of a popular soft drink.

5. How much do we misrepresent our past? After Helen dies, Warren starts to miss her and to think she was special. Is it that (a) Warren didn't know what he had until he lost it, or (b) after losing Helen he begins to imagine she was special when she really wasn't?

6. Warren says, "I know we're all pretty small in the big scheme of things, and I suppose the most you can hope for is to make some kind of difference. But what kind of difference have I made? What in the world is better because of me?" And: "Relatively soon I will die ... once I am dead and everyone who knew me dies too, it will be as though I never existed." Given these quotes, what are we to make of the last scene in which Warren cries when he sees the picture drawn by Ndugu? Is he crying from happiness because he *has* made a difference in the world? Or — as I think — is he crying because he realizes that the little bit he has done for Ndugu does not count for much? All he himself has is a drawing; and, by being human, Ndugu cannot escape the emptiness of existence.

ADDITIONAL RECOMMENDATIONS FOR
ANXIETY AND INAUTHENTICITY:

Five Easy Pieces (1970). Existentialists are "outsiders." They just don't fit in. (For an excellent portrayal of an existentialist outsider in literature, read Albert Camus' *The Stranger*.) Jack Nicholson shines as an outsider in *Five Easy Pieces*. Pay special attention to the famous chicken salad sandwich scene.

Crimes and Misdemeanors (1989). Is this Woody Allen's best film? It certainly addresses the question of whether one is happiest if one does good. Are evil people necessarily unhappy?

One Flew Over the Cuckoo's Nest (1975). Here's Jack again! There is just something about his mannerisms that express an awareness of the absurdity of all things.

5

Fate and Determinism

Chapter 4 (Anxiety and Inauthenticity) centered on the philosophical movement called "Existentialism." As stated in that chapter, most existentialists assume that all humans freely choose their essential characteristics. Humans are responsible for just about everything that happens to them. Sartre, for example, fought in the French underground during World War II and subsequently claimed that *he* was responsible for World War II. What does that mean? It means he chose to fight, and such choices are what guarantees there will be war. (If people did not choose to go to war, there would not be wars.)

The main point is that for most existentialists, people are not caused to choose what they choose and their behavior is not caused. In this chapter, we turn to a philosophy that completely rejects the notion that human individuals are free agents. We turn to "determinism." (Proponents of free will are often called "Indeterminists.")

When we say "X is determined" we mean "X is caused to occur." There are various types of determinists: hard determinists, soft determinists, and predeterminists. A predeterminist usually argues that God, at creation, set up the entire future course of the universe. Hard and soft determinists, on the other hand, have no time for some "designing creator" behind the natural chain of events.

Baron d'Holbach (1723–1789) is a famous hard determinist. D'Holbach wrote that a person is:

> born without his consent; his organization does in nowise depend
> upon himself; his ideas come to him involuntarily, his habits are in the
> power of those who cause him to contract them; he is unceasingly
> modified by causes whether visible or concealed, over which he has no
> control, which necessarily regulate his mode of existence, give the hue
> to his way of thinking and determine his manner of acting. He is good
> or bad, happy or miserable, wise or foolish, reasonable or irrational,

without his will being for anything in these various states. Nevertheless, in spite of the shackles by which he is bound, it is pretended he is a free agent or that independent of these causes by which he moved, he determines his own will, and regulates his own condition.[1]

Though d'Holbach uses the words "good" and "bad" in the above quote, determinists do not think people are responsible for their "goodness" or "badness." I would argue that determinists *can* consistently use the words "good" and "bad" in their theory. Those words are used in conformity with the utilitarian's greatest happiness principle. Adolf Hitler is "bad" because of the amount of suffering, hatred, and destruction he brought about. Mother Teresa is a better person than Hitler because she helped eliminate suffering. However, place Mother Teresa in Germany as a youth in the 1930s and she would most likely be a Nazi.

Soft determinists hold that "freedom" is not an empty word. A human being is free when he/she can do what he/she wants to do. If a wind blows me over, I would say, "I was not free to remain standing." If, when the wind blows me over, I fall on a child, killing it, I am not a bad person. However, if I want to stomp on the child and proceed to do so, I am doing what I want to do and I can rightly be judged to be doing something "bad."

It is important to note that the above use of the word "freedom" by the soft determinist does not imply anything like what most people mean by "free will" or "free agent." According to determinists, people *think* they are free agents because (a) they are ignorant of the causes of their behavior, (b) they have been programmed to think they are free, and (c) they "*feel*" they are free. (A) and (b) can be seen by considering the following: Suppose I want to buy the newest cycle of Beethoven's symphonies. I go to a CD store and find it on the shelf. I try to decide what I am going to do. Here are the "possible futures" I think I can bring about:

   i. buy the CD.
   ii. shoplift the CD.
   iii. tell the manager that I am a college professor and I will advertise his store to my undergraduates if he gives me the CD.
   iv. Buy the CD, copy it, and return the original for a refund. (Problem! Most sellers of CDs do not allow you to return a CD unless it is defective. If they have a replacement of the same CD, they will give it to you. If they don't have the same CD, they will return your money.

Therefore, you must first enter the store, hide any CD identical to the one you bought, exit the store, re-enter the store with the CD you bought and announce your CD is defective. They will look for a replacement, won't find any like it, and will give you your money back.)

    v. Buy the CD from a discount classical music club.

What happens? I am repulsed by (i) because the CD set costs $89.00. I am repulsed by (ii) because of the fear that I could get caught and lose my position as a professor at a university. I also reject (ii) because I would feel guilty if I were ever to steal anything. I don't *choose* that guilt — it comes to me. I reject (iii) because, again, I could lose my faculty position for trying to convince students to purchase CDs from a certain CD store simply because I gain material benefits from the store manager. I reject (iv) because I don't own a CD burner that will copy CDs. I choose (v) and buy the disc from a discount music club because it charges $20.00 less than the store.

Concerning (b), our teachers, clergy and parents program us when we are young to think we are free. So, whenever we are asked in our later years whether we think we are free or not, we readily say, "Of course."

The two movies discussed in this chapter offer amazingly concrete examples of what has been labeled "flukes" by a wise acquaintance. Flukes are events that are caused but have a future impact that cannot be predicted when the flukes occur. Consider the following example: In Spring 1967 I was an undergraduate student for one semester at a university in the Southwest United States. One evening I was sitting alone in the Student Union. I picked up a newspaper someone had left on a table in front of me. I paged through the newspaper. A small advertisement caught my eye: COUNSELOR WANTED, CAMP IN COLORADO. I had fallen in love with the West and did not want to return to my Pennsylvania college until absolutely necessary. But I had little money and needed a job. This camp sounded great, so I applied and was accepted. At the camp I had a wonderful time. I ended up working there for six summers. And in that first summer I met one of the cooks of the camp. A few years later I married her. Think about it! If someone had not left that newspaper on the table in the Student Union, I would not have met my wife; I would not have the children I have! Think about this: if either of your parents had sneezed while performing the sexual act, you might not have been conceived! Do you see the importance of "flukes"?

The movies you will view (*Tess* and *Sliding Doors*) also deal with another concept regularly linked with determinism — the idea that "fate" rules over people. What happens, happens by necessity, and nothing we do will change our fate. Some fatalists support the view that personal fates are pre-determined by God. Nothing in these two films indicates that God is behind events that happen to people. Our fates are what they are because of the impersonal laws of nature.

Movie 12: *Tess*

Director: Roman Polanski; 2 hours, 16 minutes; 1980

I highly recommend you read Thomas Hardy's *Tess of the d'Urbervilles* before watching the film adaptation of that work. Roman Polanski captured the plot and atmosphere of Hardy's book, but the novel is so well written and contains much more than the film.

Some years ago I visited "Thomas Hardy Country" in southern

Alec (Leigh Lawson, left) and Tess (Nastassia Kinski, right) in Roman Polanski's *Tess* (1980), based on Thomas Hardy's novel.

England, and, with the help of pamphlets published by the Hardy Society (pamphlets that guide visitors to real landmarks utilized by Hardy in his novels), I visited the village of Marnhull (which Hardy called "Marlot"), the village where Tess and her parents lived. At Marnhull I saw the cottage traditionally thought to be the one in which Hardy housed Tess, her parents, and her siblings. Nearby is the field Hardy used as the location for the dance shown at the beginning of the film. A churchyard in the village is the site where Tess buries her child. Elsewhere, I saw a dairy that may be the one Hardy called "Talbothays." Polanski did not film *Tess* at those sites, but all scenes look like the real deal. I can attest to that fact, having been there.

Watch the movie.

Questions to ponder:

1. In the film, Tess (Nastassia Kinski), explaining to Angel (Peter Firth) about Alec (Leigh Lawson) and the baby, says, "It was fate that drove me to work for false relatives as a way to help my own folk to live." Thomas Hardy was a fatalist in his novels. What does it mean to be "driven by fate"? Do you think "fate" drove Tess?

2. In the introduction to this chapter I presented the idea of "flukes." There are many "flukes" in the film and even more in the novel. For example, the note to Angel that Tess slipped under the door — it went under a rug and Angel didn't find it. List other "flukes."

Movie 13: *Sliding Doors*

Director: Peter Howitt; 1 hour, 39 minutes; 1998
Watch the movie.

Questions to ponder:

1. Did you spot the "fluke" on the steps of the subway at the beginning of the movie?

2. Do you think the two lives of Helen (Gwyneth Paltrow) are possible lives? That is, if she catches the subway, she meets James (John Hannah) and falls in love with him, but is killed by an automobile. If, however, she misses the subway, she becomes pregnant by Gerry (John Lynch) but finds out about his affair with Lydia (Jeanne Tripplehorn), falls down the stairs and loses the baby.

John Hannah and Gwyneth Paltrow in *Sliding Doors* (1998).

3. Do you think it is reasonable for the Helen who survives to have flashes from the life of Helen who did not survive? What do you take from the meeting in the elevator between Gerry and the surviving Helen?

ADDITIONAL RECOMMENDATIONS
FOR FATE AND DETERMINISM:

Run Lola Run (1999). A roller coaster-ride of a movie.

A Clockwork Orange (1971). Warning: *A Clockwork Orange* is a very disturbing movie to watch. It may ruin the famous song "Singing in the Rain" for you. Implicit in the film is a criticism of the view that a person who engages in "higher quality" pleasures will be a morally good person. (See Chapter 2: The Greatest Happiness Principle.) The main character, Alex, deeply appreciates the music of Beethoven. However, he shows that there is no connection between appreciating higher things and being a moral person. The attempt to program Alex in such a way that he cannot become violent should lead the viewer to question whether he has free will.

Blind Chance (1987). Directed by Krzysztof Kieslowski, director of *The Decalogue* (Movie 20).

6

Jesus, Muhammad, Buddha, Tammy Faye and Miscellaneous Religious Issues

I'm convinced that even the most hard-nosed atheist sometimes feels there is a supernatural divine Being, and even the most dogmatic theist has moments of doubt. Is there a God? If so, what is His nature? Is He a transcendent God who in some sense reigns over His creation? Is He an immanent God out of which all things arise? Do we think of God entirely too much in human terms? Do we create God in our image? What evidence do we have that there is *anything* other than ordinary natural things like trees, water, planets, rocks, people, etc.? Why are we often tempted to turn against what we believe to be religious truth?

The above questions, and many others, are addressed in some or all of the following seven movies. They will give you plenty to ponder.

Movie 14: *The Last Temptation of Christ*

Director: Martin Scorcese; 2 hours, 43 minutes; 1988

When *The Last Temptation of Christ* was released in 1988, it was scheduled to be shown in a city near my home town. I would have gone to see it. However, the theater received numerous threats and it wasn't shown. I had to travel 65 miles to see the movie. Entering that theater I had to pass a group of protestors. As it turned out, I was disappointed in the movie. All the disciples seemed to have Brooklyn accents. Harvey Keitel as Judas? Plus, the film was actually too traditional for my taste. Some of the lines spoken by characters are just pathetic. As Jesus (Willem Dafoe) confronts the crowd throwing stones at Mary Magdalene (Barbara Hershey), he says to one of the stone-throwers: "Be careful.... There

Willem Dafoe, as Jesus, telling those who have not sinned to cast the first stone in *The Last Temptation of Christ* **(1988).**

is a God. He's seen you cheat your workers. He's seen you with that widow…what's her name?" From the crowd off camera comes a voice calling the name "Judith."

So, I saw the film. Subsequently, a review of the movie appeared in my university newspaper. The review was written by a philosophy major — one of my students. A problem: this student had not seen the movie! He read some fundamentalist propaganda that claimed Jesus says such things as the following in the film: "Mary, God is in your sexual organs." (It is true that Mary Magdalene says to Jesus, "You want to save my soul? This is where you'll find it," as she tries to direct Jesus' hand to her sexual organs. However, this action is early in the movie before Mary accepts the fact that Jesus is the Messiah.) The student, using "information" from a propaganda sheet, told the readers of the newspaper they should stay away from the film.

Education is dead if movies that have not been seen are reviewed by campus newspaper reporters. So I arranged to take two vans of interested students to that theater 65 miles away so they could see the picture. The result was that about one-third of the students thought it was a very good movie, about one-third thought it *might* contain some blasphemous elements, and one-third thought it was just not very good.

I find the famous controversial dream sequence at the end of the film to be in good taste. I'm surprised more people weren't shocked by an early scene in which Jesus sits within view of Mary Magdalene while she plies her trade as a prostitute. He is waiting to ask her forgiveness for something. I think the probable explanation of the silence about that scene by people who criticized the dream sequence is that they had not seen the film.

Watch the movie.

Questions to ponder:

1. Well, what do you think? Is the movie blasphemous? Why or why not? What part of the movie is most questionable? What do you think about Jesus' last temptation (the dream sequence)?

2. Was Willem Dafoe a believable Jesus? Is *The Last Temptation of Christ* a better movie than traditional Hollywood portrayals of Jesus that merely restate the Biblical story of Jesus' life? Would Jesus have been more like the person portrayed in *The Last Temptation of Christ* or like those portrayed in traditional Hollywood movies?

Anyone who views *The Last Temptation of Christ* should also view Mel Gibson's *The Passion of the Christ* (2004) and vice versa. *The Passion* is a mixture of great filmmaking and bad horror movie. In the film, Jesus loses more blood than you could find in a full-grown elephant. Still, there are scenes in *The Passion* that are powerful and unforgettable. Why didn't *The Last Temptation of Christ* move the masses as much as *The Passion*? *Temptation* was criticized for including scenes not obtained from the Bible. However, *The Passion* also contains non-traditional scenes. Does *The Passion* come out ahead because of its marketing campaign? Its casting? Because Jesus is shown to suffer so much? Note: Contrary to what some overly enthusiastic parents think, young children should *not* be taken to view this movie. Children should be protected from viewing such things as the scourging of a person or a raven plucking out the eyes of someone being crucified.

Movie 15: *The Message*

Director: Moustapha Akkad; 2 hours, 30 minutes; (1976)

Since the attack on the World Trade Center, more and more Americans are aware of the need to become knowledgeable about the tenets of Islam. (The need for such knowledge was there before 9/11, but ethnocentricity has been a problem that has reared its head in American leadership circles throughout our history.)

The Message is a good starting point for those who have little or no knowledge of Islam.

Just as Jesus provides a model for behavior for Christians, Muhammad provides a model for Muslim life. In *The Message*, Muhammad passes numerous prescriptions on to his followers. It is interesting to compare many of these prescriptions with central ones from the Judeo-Christian tradition.

In the film, no actor plays Muhammad. To show Muhammad would

Anthony Quinn in *The Message* (1976).

be an offense to any Muslim. (Should Christians be offended by the Hollywood image of Jesus in epic presentations of the New Testament?) Too many actors in *The Message* are not persons from the Middle East region. Still, this film is an epic presentation on the scale of *The Ten Commandments* (1956). The only reason it is not as well-known by the general American public is, again, the existence of that all-pervasive ethnocentricity. People are interested in movies about their *own* religion. Since Islam is a minority religion in America, *The Message* does not hold the prominence it deserves.

Founders of religions tend to start their path toward enlightenment as "outsiders." What they profess will seem foreign to those programmed to accept the status quo. *The Message* captures the threat posed by Muhammad's message to the merchants and leaders of Mecca. In addition, as in ancient Israel at the time Abraham brought the word of the one true God who is to replace the multiplicity of tribal Gods, Muhammad brings the message that there is only one God, and that God is Allah.

Muhammad was a successful businessman in Mecca. Something about his nature, however, led him to the contemplative life. He would periodically withdraw from society by seeking solitude in caves on Mount Hira. By the age of 40, Muhammad received messages from Allah by way of the angel Gabriel. The collection of messages became known as *The Message*, and that collection comprises the Koran, the Muslim holy book. Anyone who wishes to know what Allah's message is for humanity should read a copy of the Koran.

Huston Smith's *The World's Religions: Our Great Wisdom Traditions* is a book I have admired for years as an excellent introduction to all the major world religions. Chapters on Christianity and Taoism provide especially exciting reading. The other chapters, including the one on Islam, are also excellent. To fill in the gaps in the account of Muhammad's life in *The Message*, read *Muhammad: A Biography of the Prophet*, by Karen Armstrong (San Francisco: Harper, 1993).

Watch the movie.

Questions to ponder:

1. In *The Message*, one person claims that what Christ says and what Muhammad says are like "rays from the same lamp." Given what you

know about Christianity and Islam, do you think that statement is true? Are Allah and the God of Jews and Christians one and the same God?

2. There are many, many gods worshipped around the world. How can one know that a particular god is the "true one"? I'm not being facetious here. How do you know the one true God is not Zeus? If you don't believe in Zeus, and Zeus is the one true God, he is going to be very angry with you! Does the fact that you are certain the God you worship is the one true God guarantee that you are correct? People who believe in a different God than you will be just as certain they are right.

3. I enjoy epics about the world religions, but one thing bothers me: the fact that life as portrayed on the screen probably differs radically from what life was *really* like when a religion was born. What elements of *The Message* do you think are unrealistic? What elements are accurate?

Movie 16: *Little Buddha*

Director: Bernardo Bertolucci; 2 hours, 3 minutes; 1994

I know, I know. Keanu Reeves as the Buddha? What's new? I'll bet most Americans are certain Moses looked like Charleton Heston.

Scores of movies have been made that portray the Biblical story of Jesus. The value of *Little Buddha* is that equal time is given to the reported life of the founder of one of the world's Far Eastern religions.

The cinematography of *Little Buddha* is ravishing, but don't expect great acting. This movie is not the highpoint in the acting career of Keanu Reeves. In addition, Chris Isaak and Bridget Fonda leave a lot to be desired as the parents of a reincarnated Tibetan Monk. For me, only one actor in the film possessed a pleasant screen presence — Ying Ruocheng as Lama Norbu.

Watch the movie.

Questions to ponder:

1. Both Jesus and Buddha claimed that they

Keanu Reeves in Bernardo Bertolucci's *Little Buddha* (1994).

had a way to redeem the world. All people, they claimed, are in need of salvation. Buddha found compassion for all things; Jesus commanded us to "love our neighbors." However, as the film makes clear, there are some fundamental differences between the views of these two religious founders. For example:

 a. Buddha taught us to meditate in order to empty our minds. Meditation is directed at no thing. Christian prayer, on the other hand, is directed towards a transcendent God. What reasons are there to think one of these methods that are to lead to salvation is better than the other?

 b. The form of Buddhism presented in *Little Buddha* includes the notion that all living things are reincarnations of past creatures. There is nothing like the Buddhist concept of reincarnation in Christianity. According to Christianity, at death our souls will be judged and we will either be permitted to enter God's heaven or be forced to go to some undesirable place. Are there good reasons to believe in either reincarnation or in the Christian afterlife?

 c. Do you believe a tree lowered a branch to help Buddha's mother as she gave birth? Or that a giant cobra used its hood to shield the meditating Siddhartha from the rain? Or that Mora tempted Siddhartha, much as Satan tempted Jesus?

Comments:

 One of the most important distinctions I have found in Philosophy is the distinction between "insiders" and "outsiders." Someone who is filled with admiration towards George W. Bush is an "insider." Such a person could not understand criticism leveled against Bush by an "outsider." The outsider could not make any sense of the insider's admiration. I love reading great classics. An outsider would think reading great classics is boring. An insider who fervently worships God will not understand Nietzsche's sentence, "God is dead." A Nietzschean could not understand the beliefs of a religious fundamentalist. If you are not a Buddhist, you are "outside" Buddhism and would think various elements of the reported life of Buddha are absurd. If you are an outsider to Christianity, the statements that, "Jesus walked on water," or that, "He rose from the dead," do not make sense. People "inside" Christianity will judge that the events just mentioned certainly happened. Thus, your answers to the questions I raised about *Little Buddha* will depend on whether you are an insider or an outsider when it comes to Buddhism.

Movie 17: *The Apostle*

Director: Robert Duvall; 2 hours, 14 minutes; 1998
Watch the movie.

Questions to ponder:

1. The car wreck scene near the beginning of *The Apostle* is a powerful portrayal of the effect a person of God can have on someone on the verge of death. However, what do you think: Did Sonny (Robert Duvall) have a right to impose himself on the young couple who were accident victims? One of the policemen at the scene said to Sonny, "I guess you think you accomplished something in there, huh?" Sonny answered, "I know I did." What, if anything, did he accomplish?

2. Would you want Sonny to be your clergy person or spiritual advisor? Why or why not?

Robert Duvall as "the Apostle E.F." in a scene from *The Apostle* (1998), written and directed by Duvall.

3. Did the Apostle truly repent the mistakes he had made, including hitting his wife's lover with a baseball bat? Late in the movie, as he prays to God to protect the church he has founded, Sonny adds, "I just pray that you'll let that man Horace live. In the name of Jesus, let him live." If he had truly repented, should he have turned himself in? He felt he had "done something" by establishing his new church. But if he had turned himself in, he could have "done something" by preaching to other prisoners in the penitentiary.

Comments:

Robert Duvall's audio commentary that accompanies the DVD of *The Apostle* is excellent. He shows a reverence for—and a deep understanding of—preachers like Sonny.

The one set of scenes that do not work for me are those that center on the Billy Bob Thornton character. I find these scenes embarrassingly bad. Thornton has been in some excellent movies. My favorite is still his first—the movie he wrote, directed, and starred in—*Sling Blade* (1997).

Movie 18: *Breaking the Waves*

Director: Lars von Trier; 2 hours, 39 minutes; 1996
Warning: Explicit sexual scenes; filmed with a hand-held camera.
Watch the movie.

Questions to ponder:

1. A colleague and a number of my female students were angered by *Breaking the Waves*. They were angered by Bess (Emily Watson), who meekly follows the orders of her husband Jan (Stellan Skarsgard). They were especially angered by Jan's request that Bess should sleep with other men. Were you angered?

2. Why do you think the title of the film is *Breaking the Waves*?

3. When Bess goes to the boat in the harbor for the second time, she knows she is putting herself in mortal danger. She is sacrificing herself to save Jan. If her sister-in-law Dodo (Katrin Cartlidge) or Dr. Richardson (Adrian Rawlins) knew what she is doing, they would stop her and institutionalize her. Would they be right to institutionalize her? Remember: if they stop her, it is highly unlikely Jan will recover! Clearly a miracle occurs as a result of Bess' sacrifice and Dodo's prayer. Another

Emily Watson and Stellan Skarsgard in Lars von Trier's *Breaking the Waves* (1996).

miracle occurs in the last scene when the bells ring from the heavens. (Maybe Bess' church has no need for bells, but God will supply them to ring for the risen Bess!) Given her love, her goodness, and her sacrifice, doesn't it make sense to interpret Bess to be "Christ-like"?

4. If you agree with my interpretation as implied in the preceding question, does it not follow that when Bess talks to God, it is indeed God who answers? If it is God speaking and only Bess hears God's message, then only Bess can make sense of what she is doing. Note the similarity with the Old Testament story of Abraham. Abraham is willing to sacrifice his son Isaac because he is commanded to do so by God. But Abraham does not tell his wife or neighbors what he is planning to do because they might try to stop him *they* have not heard God's voice. Viewers will see Bess' sexual activity as obscene. But is what she is willing to do any less obscene than what Abraham was willing to do? Neither Bess nor Abraham *wants* to do what God orders them to do. God willed that His son, Jesus, be crucified. Jesus had nails driven into his hands. He willingly accepted that torture. Is that more understandable than Bess' sacrifice?[1]

Movie 19: *The Eyes of Tammy Faye*

Directors: Fenton Bailey and Randy Barbato; 1 hour, 20 minutes; 1999

People who are too young to remember the 1980s will not realize just how much Jim and Tammy Bakker were household names. Their followers were legion. Their story is amazing.

Watch the movie.

Questions to ponder:

1. At the beginning of the film, Tammy Faye says, "I think the eyes are so important — I believe [eyes] are the eyes of the soul. I truly do. And I think you can look inside someone's eyes and really tell what kind

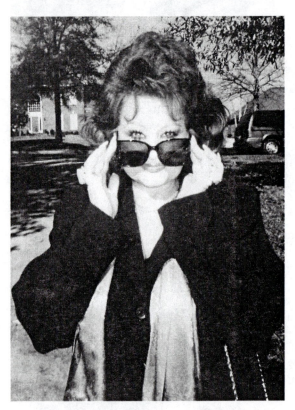

Behind the sunglasses are *The Eyes of Tammy Faye* (1999).

of person and what their heart is [*sic*]." What do *you* see in Tammy Faye's eyes?

2. The "performances" of Jim and Tammy Faye seem so hokey. (Or do you disagree?) Why would anyone think they speak for God?

3. In the 1980s I would periodically turn on *The PTL Club* just to see what Tammy would cry about next. I knew she was on something — pills or something else. However, I was genuinely moved by many parts of her story in *The Eyes of Tammy Faye*. Were you moved? Why? Why would a non-believer be moved by

such things as Tammy Faye getting to sing once again on TV or signing an autograph for the reporter who broke the story of the corruption in Jim Bakker's *PTL Club?*

Movie 20: *The Decalogue*

Director: Krzysztof Kieslowski; 9 hours, 30 minutes; 1988

You are about to watch one of the greatest cinematic masterpieces of all time — ten hour-long films made for Polish television in the 1980s by the great director Krzysztof Kieslowski. Given extremely limited release in theaters due to the length of *The Decalogue*, few people outside of Poland have been exposed to its wonders. Fortunately, in 1999 it was finally released as a set of three DVDs.

Each film centers on one of the Ten Commandments. Roger Ebert, however, has written that viewers would waste a "lot of time trying to match up the films and the commandments. There isn't a one-to-one correlation; some films touch on more than one commandment."[2] I agree with Ebert that at times more than one commandment is being addressed. Still, I think it was not an accident that Kieslowski picked a single commandment as a label for each movie.

Shot in some semi-ghetto locale, the films present "a satiric view of crumbling Polish society in the new age of greed."[3] The screenplays are by Kieslowski and his co-writer Krzystof Piesiewicz. A different cinematographer lensed each episode. Major characters from one film show up fleetingly in others.

Be sure to notice the strange young man who appears in most of the episodes. He doesn't say anything — he simply looks at someone who plays an important part in the film. I call him "the looker." Most of the time I think the looker is peering at someone who is about to break the commandment around which the film is centered. Roger Ebert has presented one interpretation of the looker that I think is right on target:

> There is a young man who appears in eight [of the films], a solemn onlooker who never says anything but sometimes makes eye contact. I thought perhaps he represented Christ, but Kieslowski, in an essay about the series, says, "I don't know who he is; just a guy who comes and watches us, our lives." He's not very pleased with us.... I like the theory of Annette Insdorf in her valuable book about Kieslowski, *Double Lives, Second Chances*; she compares the watcher to the angels in

Wim Wender's *Wings of Desire* (1988) who are "pure gaze"—able to "record human folly and suffering but unable to alter the course of the lives they witness."[4]

After viewing *The Decalogue* it is very rewarding to watch the film Ebert mentioned above—*Wings of Desire*.

Decalogue I: "I am the Lord, thy God; thou shalt not have other Gods before me."

Watch the movie.

Questions to ponder:

1. The aunt (Maja Komorowska) believes in God. She says to the boy (Wojciech Klata) about his father (Henryk Baranowski): "Measurements (can) be applied to everything.... Your dad's way of life may seem more reasonable, but it doesn't rule out God." Is the computer a false god worshipped by the father?

2. Does the father take all the necessary steps in determining whether or not it is safe to skate on the ice? He performs his calculations, walks on the ice, hits it with a stick, and jumps on it. He says, "The ice couldn't break." Does this section indicate he has a "false god"? After taking all those precautions, is there anything about which he should feel guilty?

Comments:

The child asks his aunt, "What is God?" She gives him a hug and says, "*That's* where he is." Her remark captures the central theme found in Martin Buber's classic work *I and Thou*. For the most part, we treat things and people as things to be manipulated for selfish purposes. When we do that, according to Buber, we are in an "I—it" relationship. When we authentically relate to something or someone, we are in an "I—Thou" relationship, a relationship of love. God is present when we enter into an "I—Thou" relationship because God *is* relation, God is love.[5] (I will return to Buber's "I—it" and "I—Thou" distinction in my presentation of Movie 70, *Babette's Feast*.)

Decalogue II: "Thou shalt not take the name of the Lord thy God in vain."

Watch the movie.

Questions to ponder:

1. Do you think this episode centered on the second commandment? If so, how?

2. Why did the physician (Aleksander Bardini) lie to the wife (Krystyna Janda) by saying her husband would die? Big hint: She was considering an abortion if her husband died, and the physician's children had died in some devastating accident.

3. Here is a question about something easy to miss in the film. The wife brings a jar of berries for her husband. She starts to leave with the jar. The other patient in the room says, "Leave it. He may eat it later." Subsequently, that patient dies. Later, the jar is shown again. Most of the berries have been eaten. Was there a connection between the patient's death and the berries the wife left?

Decalogue III: "Remember the Sabbath day, to keep it holy."

Watch the movie.

A question to ponder:

1. Edward, the secret lover of Eva (Maria Pakulnis) is out of the picture. Janusz (Daniel Olbrychski) clearly loves his wife, but also has not forgotten Eva, his lover of three years before. Was it fair of Eva to take Janusz away from his family on Christmas Eve so her life would feel "normal"?

Decalogue IV: "Honor thy father and thy mother."

Watch the movie.

Questions to ponder:

1. Did Michael (Janusz Gajos) have a good reason for not showing Anka (Adrianna Biedrynska) the letter from her mother? Did Anka have the right to see it? Did she do anything wrong in opening it and reading it?

2. Michael has been such a good father to Anka. Given her reaction on finding out he is not her real father, would it have been best for Michael to destroy the letter years before?

3. Why did Michael and Anka burn the letter?

4. After Anka learns that Michael is not her real father, she says she always suspected it and implies she always had a great desire to become physically close to him. She says that when she made love to someone else she thought of Michael. Is she telling the truth? If not, why does she say such things?

Decalogue V: "Thou shalt not kill."

Warning: A very violent scene, plus other intense scenes!
Watch the movie.

A question to ponder:
Jacek (Misoslaw Baka) killed the taxi driver (Jan Tesarz) in cold blood. He showed no remorse about the murder. In spite of those facts, does the film make a case against capital punishment? Is the execution of Jacek any different in appearance in any substantial way from the murder of the taxi driver?

Comments:
In Chapter 5, I mentioned details in a person's life that I call "flukes"— seemingly insignificant events that unexpectedly lead to major events. In this episode of *The Decalogue*, a number of flukes lead to Jacek murdering this particular taxi driver and not another driver. For example, the taxi driver plays a dirty trick on Dorota and her husband (characters from *Decalogue II*, the one in which the husband is dying and Dorota is deciding whether or not to have an abortion). He is waxing the taxi cab and they wait for him to finish so he can give them a ride. However, just to be nasty, the cabby drives off without them. If he had taken them to their destination, it is improbable he would have picked up Jacek. Also, the taxi driver refuses to pick up a drunk. Had he picked up the drunk, Jacek would not have been his passenger. In addition, Jacek, after his arrest, tells the lawyer (Krzysztof Globisz) he probably would not have become a murderer if his sister had not accidentally been killed.

Decalogue VI: "Thou shalt not commit adultery."

This episode is Kieslowski at his best. Though there is no murder involved, numerous scenes in *Decalogue VI* are reminiscent of Hitchcock's *Rear Window* in which James Stewart spies on neighbors. While the plots differ, Kieslowski's film should be considered just as much a landmark of cinema as Hitchcock's.

Watch the movie.

Questions to ponder:

1. Do you find Tomak (Olaf Lubaszenko) likeable? After all, he is a peeping tom and he steals letters from the mailbox of Magda (Grazyna Szapolowska).

2. Why did Tomak attempt suicide?

3. Magda believed love was merely something physical. Did Tomak convince her she was wrong? If so, how?

4. At the end of the film, Tomak proclaims that he no longer peeps at Magda. Why has he changed so much?

Decalogue VII: "Thou shalt not steal."

Watch the movie.

Questions to ponder:

1. Why did Wojtek (Boguslaw Linda) help Ewa (Anna Polony) track down Majka (Maja Barelkowska) when Majka left her house with her daughter? Was he right to do so? Did he fear that Majka might commit suicide and harm her daughter?

2. Did Majka's father (Wladyslaw Kowalski) do enough to help Majka in her plight?

3. Why did Majka's daughter have nightmares and scream while sleeping? Was Wojtek correct when he said she was afraid of what the future would bring?

Decalogue VIII: "Thou shalt not bear false witness against your neighbor."

Watch the movie.

Questions to ponder:

1. Professor Zofia (Maria Koscialkowska) says there is nothing more important than a child. And yet, to protect the activities of her husband and others in the underground movement, she sends Elzbieta (Teresa Marczewska) away. Is she being consistent? Or has she changed her view?

A scene from *Decalogue IX* (1988), starring Ewa Błaszczyk as Hanka (left) and Piotr Machalica as Roman (right).

Is she saying that if she had it to do over again, she would not send Elzbieta away: Would that action be the right thing to do?

2. Professor Zofia is a philosophy professor. She does not tell her students how to live, but rather that they should "discover themselves." Socrates is famous for emphasizing the prescription "Know thyself." What does it mean to discover or know yourself? Is it more important to know yourself or to know how to live? Why?

***Decalogue IX:* "Thou shalt not covet they neighbor's wife."**

Watch the movie.

Questions to ponder:

1. Roman (Piotr Machalica) tells Hanka (Ewa Blaszczyk): "[You will] have to start seeing somebody if you haven't already." Well, she has already been seeing someone — Marusz (Artur Barcis). Is Roman really giving Hanka permission to have an affair? If not, what motivates him to say she should have one?

2. Hanka clearly loves Roman. By choice, she breaks off the affair with Marusz. She clearly does not enjoy having sexual relations with Marusz. Given those facts, is Roman's constant spying despicable? When she finds out what he has been doing, Hanka shows more sadness than anger. Should she have been angry, sad, or both? Why?

Decalogue X: "Thou shalt not covet they neighbor's goods."

Watch the movie.

Questions to ponder:

1. What characteristics distinguish a healthy relationship with material goods and an unhealthy attachment? Which of those characteristics pertain to Jerzy (Jerzy Stuhr) and Artur (Zbigniew Zamachowski) and their attitudes toward their father's stamp collection?

2. After the invaluable stamp collection is stolen, you would think Jerzy and Artur would be crushed. But in the last scenes they seem happy. How can that condition be explained?

An additional question about the whole series of *Decalogue* episodes:

1. My favorite episode is Number 9. What is yours? Why? What is your least favorite episode? Why?

ADDITIONAL RECOMMENDATIONS FOR
MOVIES ON RELIGIOUS THEMES:

The Passion of Joan of Arc (1928). One of the greatest movies ever made? Critics rave about Carl Meyer's direction and the acting of Renee Falconetti. I can't see what all the fuss is about. But you should judge for yourself.

Ben Hur (1959). As time has moved on, the acting seems dated. The special effects, particularly of the sea flight, seem amateurish. Still, *Ben Hur* is a compelling story that can move you. The chariot race remains one of the great sequences in film history.

Inherit the Wind (1960). From the play by Jerome Lawrence and Robert E. Lee. This is a fictionalized account of the great "Monkey Trial" of 1925. A school teacher breaks a Tennessee law against teaching evolution in schools and is brought to trial. Spencer Tracy defends the school teacher and Fredric Marsh is the prosecuting attorney. The

roles Tracy and Marsh play are based on the historical personages
Clarence Darrow and William Jennings Bryan. The actual "Monkey Trial" was definitely one of the great trials of the 20th century.

Barrabas (1962). Par Lagerkvist, the Nobel Prize–winning author, wrote
the novel *Barrabas* about the fictional life of the man who was to be
crucified but was replaced by Jesus. That short novel would be an
excellent read before viewing the film.

The Gospel According to St. Matthew (1964). This film follows the traditional tale of Jesus. There is the virgin birth, the miracles performed
by Jesus, and the crucifixion. However, the human side of Jesus
stands out. An excellent musical score enriches the viewing experience.

The Exorcist (1973). One of the scariest movies ever made. The viewer
will believe a demonic possession has taken place.

Jesus of Nazareth (1977). At over six hours in length, director Franco
Zeffirelli made a valiant attempt at a complete and accurate re-telling
of the New Testament stories of Jesus. *Jesus of Nazareth* was origi-
nally produced for television.

Monty Python's The Life of Brian (1979). So blasphemous — but, oh, so funny.

Agnes of God (1985). Based on a Broadway play. There is excellent acting by Meg Tilly, Jane Fonda and Anne Bancroft. The first half of
the film sets up a chilling scenario. The second half is a bit of a letdown.

The Rapture (1991). Captures the power of conversion and the dangers
of excessive religious conviction.

Not Without My Daughter (1991). A very controversial film. When
released, this film offended many members of the Islamic faith. Based
on a true story, but the story is probably one-sided. There is too
much stereotyping. Still, it is not a boring movie.

Priest (1995). Warning: Contains a number of elements that may shock
some viewers.

A Life Apart: Hasidism in America (1997). A documentary that helps the
viewer understand and appreciate a religious group usually only seen
from the outside.

Dogma (1999). A controversial satire. My students rave about this film.
I was turned off by the acting of Matt Damon, Ben Affleck, and Chris
Rock. Particularly dull for me were scenes in which the popular
singer Alanis Morissette plays God.

7

The Journey Upward

What was Martin Luther King, Jr., saying when he claimed he had "been to the mountaintop?" Whatever it was, it included the notions that (a) getting to the mountaintop will not occur without great struggle and opposition, and (b) reaching that goal is a defining, awe-inspiring moment in a person's life.

The courageous overcoming of forces that tend to keep a person down can be found in the works of numerous great philosophers. On the first page of Friedrich Nietzsche's *Thus Spake Zarathustra*, the fictional Zarathustra leaves his home and goes into the mountains and becomes wise. Though Nietzsche greatly appreciated the solitude and clean air of the mountains, he does not restrict the phrase "climbing mountains" to the mere climbing of physical mountains. Nietzsche climbed mountains by writing his books — books that conveyed ideas that could not be comprehended by most people. He climbed mountains by being daringly original. Martin Luther King, Jr., clearly had not climbed a physical mountain just prior to his famous speech.

The best philosophical source for the idea of rising above pettiness or ignorance to become a wise person is Plato's famous "Allegory of the Cave" from his *Republic*. In this allegory, Plato describes people chained from childhood in a cave. They can only look straight ahead at the wall of the cave. Behind them a fire burns, the fire providing a source of light. In front of the fire, but behind the chained human beings, there is a "road along which a low wall has been built, as the exhibitors of puppet shows have partitions before the men themselves, above which they show puppets." Men walk behind the wall holding up "implements of all kinds" and "human images and shapes of animals as well, wrought in stone and wood and every material." Shadows of those "implements," "human images" and "shapes" are cast onto the wall in front of the prisoners. Those shadows are what they see day after day. Prisoners give names to the shadows and "deem reality to be nothing else than the shadows." Plato then has us imagine what happens if the chains of one individual are removed and that person is forced to look around. The experience would be painful. If he were then to ascend from the cave into the light of the sun, he would be blinded. Finally, however, his sight would clear. And the world would show itself in all its beauty. If he returned to the cave, he could not at first adjust to the darkness of the cave, and other prisoners would laugh at him. In fact, if he tries to help them leave the cave, they would feel threatened by the man who has discovered something other than their shadow world; and "if it were possible to lay hands on and to kill the man," they would.[1]

There are certainly elements of Plato's Cave that would not ordinarily find their way into movies. For Plato, what is outside the cave is literally some world other than our present world of space and time. Outside the cave is a world of perfect Forms, the eternal essences of things. Forms do not exist in our spatial-temporal world. There are Forms of Goodness (symbolized by the sun in the allegory), Justice, Perfect Triangularity, Dogness, and so forth. (In the fifth century, Augustine christianized Plato's philosophy. For Augustine, what is outside the cave is the realm of the Christian God.)

The elements of the allegory that are captured in movies include the notion that the masses of people are often brainwashed by powerful persons and forces. Mass media, for example, is often accused of manipulating the minds of ordinary people (see *Network* [1976], for example). Perhaps it is religious indoctrination that "chains" people, an example of which can be seen in *Breaking the Waves* (Movie 18) in its characterization of the power the Church Elders hold over their flock.

Those who are manipulated often do not realize they lack freedom and lack knowledge. They will think the "shadows" they see constitute "reality." A person who attempts to break free will be seen as a dangerous pervert by those satisfied by their state of ignorance. (Thus Nietzsche prescribes: "Live dangerously.") People who leave the cave may face the end that Socrates and Jesus received (execution), or that Martin Luther King, Jr., and Gandhi encountered (assassination). Often, however, those who struggle to rise above will merely be met with ostracism and scorn.

In Chapters 4 and 5 I discuss the concept of "free will." The freedom experienced by one who leaves the cave or climbs the mountain is not the same concept as that of "free will." I find the former freedom to be much more meaningful than the notion of free will. The exhilaration of someone who, after facing unbelievably difficult obstacles, rises up out of some lowly state and is "free"— no longer a slave or "prisoner of the cave"— points to one of the most meaningful elements of life. On the mountain heights, depth is discovered. In the cave or valley is where shallowness and slavery reside. As Albert Camus put it, "The struggle to the heights is enough to fill a man's soul."[2]

The movies in this chapter center on the struggle to scale the mountaintop — the achievement of glorious freedom — against all odds. In several of the movies, the person who wins freedom receives help from one or more persons. In Plato's work, a prisoner is dragged out of the cave by someone trying to help him. *Billy Elliot* and *The Color Purple* provide excellent examples of people who help others achieve a state of freedom. In movies like *The Matrix* the strength to overcome obstacles resides completely in the person who is engaged in the struggle.

Movie 21: *Billy Elliot*

Director: Stephen Daldry; 1 hour, 50 minutes; 2000

Most viewers of *Billy Elliot* will be enthralled. Others will say they've seen the plot before in other movies. If you do get into the film, you will wonder how anyone could fail to not be moved by the dynamic acting of Jamie Bell and other members of the cast.

Classic rock songs such as "Get It On" by T. Rex, and The Clash's "London Calling," provide excellent atmosphere for relevant scenes.

Watch the movie.

Questions to ponder:

1. Do you believe Billy (Jamie Bell) would actually be accepted into the ballet school? Does it really matter?

2. Doesn't *Billy Elliot* show that people who appreciate "higher" things (such as ballet) will tend to be happier than those who lack such an appreciation? Think of what Billy's life would be if Mrs. Wilkerson (Julie Walters) had not taken him under her wing, or if his father (Gary Lewis) had not realized it was his duty to help Billy. Think what his father and brother would have missed if they had not experienced Billy's performance in *Swan Lake*. That experience *had* to be a high point in their lives.

Billy Elliot (Jamie Bell) as boxer turned ballet dancer.

3. Mrs. Wilkerson is the one who pulls Billy "out of the cave." What
is it that leads some people to offer a great amount of time and effort in
helping someone get on their feet? (Plato held that the true "lover" is one
who helps a person leave the cave. The "lover" is acting like the god of
love, Eros, who leads individuals to the Good. See Plato's famous dialogue *Symposium* for more on Eros and the nature of the authentic lover.)

4. If you are reading this book and viewing the wonderful movies
covered, or if you are engaged in some other fulfilling activities scorned
by masses of people, it is highly probable you were influenced in a pos-
itive way by some person(s) in the past. Can you identify any such per-
son(s)? Have you thanked those who have helped you grow? If not, get
on the ball! After he is accepted into the ballet school, Billy thanks Mrs.
Wilkerson. However, she does not appear at the Opera House in the last
scene to view Billy's performance. Was she still alive? Was she invited?
Is this a gap in continuity?

Movie 22: *Girlfight*

Director: Karyn Kusama; 1 hour, 50 minutes; 2001
Watch the movie.

Michelle Rodriguez (left) and Jaime Tirelli in *Girlfight* (2001).

Questions to ponder.

1. Diana (Michelle Rodriguez) doesn't get any respect. Her father (Paul Calderon) drove her mother to suicide and now constantly hovers over Diana as a physical threat. She does not have any teacher in her high school who sees promise in her. Her high school friends lack the ability to help her grow as a person. She lives in a ghetto. She notices that boxers get respect. That fact, plus a propensity to use her fists to solve problems, leads her to decide to take up boxing. Over the course of the film we come to sympathize with Diana and cheer for her. We want her to overcome her anger. Has she truly grown by the end of the movie? Would the respect a person like Diana receives for climbing into the ring provide deep meaning for that person? Or, as John Stuart Mill might claim (see Chapter 2 — The Greatest Happiness Principle), would boxing merely provide a "pigpen pleasure" that cannot truly fulfill a person? Her coach, Hector (Jaime Tirelli), says the guys in his gym have nothing other than boxing. Doesn't that indicate that, even for Hector, boxing is a poor substitute for the pleasures experienced by those who are not from economically depressed areas?

2. One of the attractive things about many films in which charac-

ters make the "journey upward" is the amazing effort exerted by those characters. As Hector puts it, being a successful boxer requires "a real strong will." The training Diana undergoes is impressive, and the viewer admires her effort. (Think of Rocky Balboa jogging through the streets of Philadelphia and boxing the sides of meat in the warehouse.) Is it *that* effort that leads Diana to respect herself and leads us to respect her? If the answer is "yes," doesn't that indicate what each viewer should do in order to gain respect — set up challenges that require "a real strong will" and great effort? In fact, Diana's boyfriend, Adrian (Santiago Douglas), says about being in the ring: "You're all you got. You're all alone in there." So many people feel they must fit into a crowd. Shouldn't they set goals for themselves that require them to perform alone in some way? By being alone and facing challenges, a person gets to know him/herself. Hector asks Diana, "Inside, do you know yourself?" Diana says she does. Hector smiles and says, "That's all you need." Does Diana know herself in ways that, for example, Marisol (Elisa Bocanegra), her friend from high school, does not know herself? What does she have that Marisol does not?

3. Are you convinced that the love Diana finds with Adrian will fulfill her in the future? Adrian needs to be a professional boxer, and being beaten by Diana destroyed that dream. That's why he said, "Satisfied?" at the end of the bout. What I am implying with my question can be clarified by thinking of the major shift in plot from Act 1 to Act 2 of Stephen Sondheim's *Into the Woods*. At the end of Act 1, famous fairy tale characters, including Rapunzel and Cinderella, "live happily ever after" — at least until Act 2 when the rest of the story unfolds. Marital infidelity and other events contrary to happy living occur in that act. My question about Diana and Adrian may be unfair because it is the type of question that could be asked about any cinematic romance. But do Diana and Adrian have enough of a foundation to guarantee their love will continue long into the future?

Movie 23: *The Truman Show*

Director: Peter Weir; 1 hour, 43 minutes; 1998

Jim Carrey is excellent as Truman, but his performance is not as much a breaking-away from the style of his comedy films as many have claimed. Ed Harris is convincing as a conniving semi-god named

Christof. The current avalanche of reality TV shows adds credibility to *The Truman Show*. There are real people who would do what Christof does if they could.

Notice Truman's reference to "going to the top of the mountain" in a scene that appears in the midst of the opening credits.

After viewing the film, if you want to see another movie that shares many of the same themes, see *Pleasantville* (1998).

Watch the movie.

Questions to ponder.

1. Truman's "friend," Marlon (Noah Emmerich), says, "It's all true. It's all real. Nothing here is false. Nothing you see on the show is fake. It's merely controlled." Do you agree with Morton's assessment? Was he *really* Truman's friend? Why or why not?

2. Why doesn't Truman want to leave the island earlier? Does he need clues, like the unexpected reappearance of his "dad"—clues that show Sea Haven life is not all it seems to be — in order to be able to make the choice to leave? Few people who are programmed to accept a certain lifestyle choose to rebel and follow a different path. Does the explana-

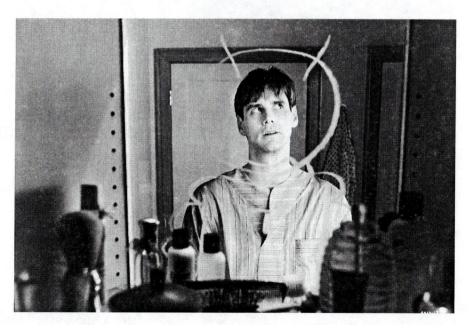

Jim Carrey stars in *The Truman Show* (1998).

tion for this lack of rebellion lie in the fact that clues showing different options are missing? Christof says, "We accept the reality of the world with which we are presented." Plato's cave dwellers are only presented a world of shadows. Truman is merely given the world of the island. Are there similar reasons behind the cave dwellers not leaving the cave and Truman not leaving the island earlier?

3. Christof says, "Sea Haven is the way the world should be." Is he correct? Is the world we now live in, in *any* way like Sea Haven?

4. Is the fear experienced by Truman as he faces the door that opens to the real world like the fear, mentioned by Plato, that arises in leaving the cave?

Movie 24: *The Matrix*

Keanu Reeves in *The Matrix* (1999).

Directors: Larry and Andy Wachowski; 2 hours, 19 minutes; 1999

I am not into special effects action movies. After all these years, I still remember the disgust I felt as I viewed scenes from *Batman* movies, scenes of Danny deVito playing the Penguin, Michelle Pfeiffer as Catwoman, Jack Nicholson as the Joker, Tommy Lee Jones as Two-Face, Jim Carrey as the Riddler, and Arnold Schwarzenegger as Mr. Freeze. Though as a child I loved Spiderman comic books, I was bored by the 2002 film. *The Incredible Hulk* was one of my favorite TV shows when I was a young whippersnapper. But the 2003 movie turned the Hulk into a big hunk of nutty putty that could jump and bounce hundreds of feet into the air. Additionally, I do not like seeing movie heroes unrealistically killing hundreds of enemies while they themselves come out of the fights relatively unscathed. The *Rambo* movies are prime examples of this excess. In short, I would rather have the Flash Gordon serials of the middle 20th century that utilized pathetic special effects than the overblown, bombastic, in-your-face fx FX that permeate films of the last few decades. However, there are exceptions, *The Matrix* is one of them!

In *The Matrix*, Neo (Keanu Reeves), Morpheus (Laurence Fishburne) and Trinity (Carrie-Anne Moss) are superheroes. The villains, notably Agents Smith (Hugo Weaving), Brown (Paul Goddard) and Jones (Robert Taylor), are distractingly reminiscent of the Blues Brothers. But originality and unique special effects enable the film to transcend the elements that ordinarily clutter action movies. Even if you are turned off by special effects movies, give *The Matrix* a chance. Lighten up, sit back, and enjoy!

Watch the movie.

Questions to ponder:

1. Did you spot the obvious references to Plato's Cave? For example, consider the following exchange from the movie:

> MORPHEUS: The Matrix is " "the world that has been pulled over your eyes to blind you from the truth...."
> NEO: What truth?
> MORPHEUS: That you are a slave, Neo. Like everyone else, you were born into bondage, born into a prison that you cannot smell or taste or touch. A prison for your mind.

2. In his great work *Meditations*, René Descartes attempted to doubt everything in order to discover truths that cannot be doubted. As you will see in the following quote, Descartes held that we are often led astray by our faulty senses. In addition, when we *think* we are really sensing something, we may indeed be dreaming.

> All that up to the present time I have accepted as most true and certain I have learned either from the senses or through the senses; but it is sometimes proved to me that these senses are deceptive, and it is wiser not to trust entirely to any thing by which we have once been deceived...

In addition, I must remember that I am a man, and that consequently I am in the habit of sleeping, and in my dreams representing to myself (things that are not there).... How often has it happened to me that in the night I dreamt that I found myself in this particular place, that I was dressed and seated near the fire, whilst in reality I was lying undressed in bed! At this moment it does indeed seem to me that it is with eyes awake that I am looking at this paper; that this head which I move is not asleep, that it is deliberately and of set purpose that I extend my hand and perceive it; what happens in sleep does not appear so clear nor so distinct as does all this. But in thinking over this I remind myself that on many occasions I have in sleep been deceived by similar illusions and in dwelling carefully on this reflection I see so manifestly that there are no certain indications by which we may clearly distinguish wakefulness from sleep that I am lost in astonishment. And my astonishment is such that it is almost capable of persuading me that I now dream.[3]

Have you ever had a dream that seemed so real you could swear what you were experiencing was not a dream? Some of you men have perhaps had such dreams! I have had some amazing dreams. Here is an account of the best one: Decades ago, I was a graduate student at the University of Delaware. I roomed with a huge, powerful football player. At that time, I was engaged. My fiancée was a dietetic intern at Massachusetts General Hospital in Boston. Day in and day out I wanted so much to be with her. Although we didn't have much money, she once visited me in Delaware. Another time I hitchhiked from Delaware to Boston. Several times we met at her aunt and uncle's house in New Jersey. We constantly tried to find ways to get together. One night I was sleeping in the apartment at the University of Delaware. The football player was sleeping in a bed across the room. I started dreaming. I dreamt I was watching TV and a commercial came on. The commercial was for an airline offering free flights to Boston! "Just come to the airport for your free flight!" Well … I went to the airport and I got on the airplane and the flight began. At the time I didn't know it, but I was almost certainly moving around the bedroom with my arms out like wings — flying. Eventually, the captain announced, "We will be landing in Boston soon. If you look out the windows you will see the lights of Boston." I looked, and I saw the lights. In fact, way down there I saw my fiancée. She was asleep. I decided to surprise her! I would land on her! I did it! I landed (jumped) on the football player! He awoke very quickly, grabbed me, and literally threw me across the room. He came after me, stood over me and yelled, "What were you doing?" (He thought he was a victim of a homosexual assault!) I started to wake up, but all I could say was, "They said it was okay on TV." Eventually, we both realized I had been dreaming and sleepwalking, and we had a good laugh.

Since in the above dream I was certain I was awake, isn't it possible that right now, though I am certain I am awake, I am really dreaming? I was certain before and I was wrong. Therefore, it follows that being certain of anything is no guarantee you are right. Can you *prove* you are not dreaming? Might you not be dreaming that you are trying to prove that you are not dreaming?

Here's what Morpheus says in *The Matrix*: "Have you ever had a dream, Neo, that you were so sure was real? What if you were unable to wake from that dream? How would you know the difference between the dream and the real world?" How can *you* tell the difference between dreaming X and really perceiving X? Whatever you list as characteristics of a waking state, are those characteristics compatible with dream states?

3. Morpheus says to Neo: "What is real? How do you define 'real'? If you are talking about what you can feel, what you can smell, what you can taste and see, then 'real' is simply electrical signals interpreted by your brain." If what you think is a perception is really some brain event, couldn't that brain event occur merely because your brain is being manipulated by some unknown intelligent being?

4. Cypher (Joe Pantoliano) is the Judas of the movie. (Morpheus is John the Baptist and Neo is the Jesus figure.) Cypher is sick of the real world. The unreal steak is too good to pass up. Cypher chooses the unreal world with its pleasures over the dismal state of affairs in the real world. This scenario suggests an idea that has been popping up in lots of philosophical discussions: the idea of a "happiness machine." Here is one presentation of that idea:

> Suppose that you had the opportunity to step into a "happiness machine" that would give you any experiences you desired. While in the machine, neurophysiologists would stimulate your brain so that, for example, you would think and feel you were winning an athletic event, writing a great novel, making a friend, or enjoying some physically and psychologically satisfying experience. To avoid boredom, the quality and types of happiness would be varied. Whatever types of experiences bring you happiness or pleasure in real life would be simulated in your brain. All the time that you are enjoying a life of uninterrupted happi-

ness, you would be floating in a tank with electrodes attached to your brain.[4]

What reason(s) would you give for *not* stepping into the "happiness machine?" After all, don't all humans seek pleasure and desire to avoid pain? Wouldn't Cypher be *wise* to go along with Agent Smith? After all, that (unreal) steak sure tastes good!

Movie 25: *The Color Purple*

Director: Steven Spielberg; 2 hours, 34 minutes; 1985

Alice Walker's novel *The Color Purple* is a contemporary masterpiece. The main character, Celie, keeps a diary. Early entries of the diary show the writer as an abused, tormented person. As she grows, the language she uses displays more and more self-assurance. Events in her life are vividly presented. The reader experiences the "lows" of Celie's life and rejoices when she makes glorious steps to improve her condition. Another character, Shug Avery, is unforgettable in her devotion to help Celie grow.

Whoopi Goldberg in her starring role as Celie in *The Color Purple* (1985).

Steven Spielberg blew it. He had material from Walker's novel that should have easily been transferable to the screen — as long as its spirit wasn't tampered with. Where Spielberg went wrong was in his addition to the film version of numerous disgusting slapstick scenes. One character falls through a roof into lower floors — twice. Danny Glover, playing Mister, the demonic husband of Celie (Whoopi Goldberg), is so determined to make the kitchen stove hotter that he pours kerosene on the flames. Of course, neither Mister nor the person who falls through the roof gets hurt. There are too many scenes like those two, and too many silly lines stuck into dialogue merely to elicit laughs. One could rightfully wonder if Spielberg really wanted to make a comedy out of Walker's novel. *The Color Purple* should be as serious a story as *Schindler's List*. It would have been as inappropriate for the latter to contain scenes of slapstick as it is for *The Color Purple*. (Some might say the same about Movie 49, *Life Is Beautiful*, but that film was created to contain slapstick.)

In spite of the above, however, *The Color Purple* offers many powerful scenes. Desreta Jackson is excellent early in the film as the young Celie, while Whoopi Goldberg is perfectly cast as the older Celie.

Watch the movie.

Questions to ponder:

1. Did you catch the explanation of the title *The Color Purple* in something Shug Avery (Margaret Avery) says? It is easy to miss in the movie, but stands out in the novel. In the novel, Shug asks Celie if she knows what would piss God off. The answer: To be walking near a field of purple flowers and not notice the color purple. Even though I am not a theist, Shug's message is a stunning one. Do you think it is stunning? Why?

2. Though parts of the movie are overdone, the scene in which Celie announces she is going with Shug to Memphis, and in which she finally stands up to Mister, is very moving. As she asserts herself, Sofia (Oprah Winfrey) says, "Settin' in that jail down there I done 'bout rot to death. I know what it like, Miss Celie, wanna go somewhere and can't. I know what it like — wanna sang — have it beat outcha." As Celie continues to express her rebellion against Mister, Sofia undergoes a radical transformation — she returns to the personality she had before she was sent to jail. Is that rapid transformation believable? Was the transformation in Celie believable? (In the novel, it certainly is!) What do you think of the transformation in Mister as he goes to the Immigration Office to help get Celie's sister and her children permission to enter the United States?

3. Before Celie leaves to accompany Shug to Memphis, Mister tells Celie, "Look at you! You're black. You're poor. You're ugly. You're a

woman. You're nothing at all." When Celie drives off, she proudly yells back to Mister, "I'm poor, Black, I may even be ugly. But, dear God, I'm here! I'm here!" She mentions all the characteristics Mister had mentioned, except that she is a woman. Should she have included that characteristic? Why?

4. The novel includes an occasion when Shug and Celie have very intimate physical contact. Shug is showing Celie that she is lovable and not ugly. In the film, Shug merely gives Celie a kiss. I found the episode in the novel to be particularly moving. Celie is experiencing the first bit of affection since her sister, Nettie, was driven away years before. Should Spielberg have included the fuller version of Shug showing Celie affection? Why or why not?

8

Civil Disobedience

Governments should work in the interest of their citizens. If a particular government engages in some activities that are not in the interest of its citizens, what should those oppressed citizens do? What if Citizen A has a duty to do "x," but "x" conflicts with the laws prescribed by his government? Suppose Citizen A is opposed not only by the members of the government but also by a significant number of other citizens. Failure to change the law is a very real possibility. It is unlikely Citizen A will successfully use persuasion to change the minds of those opposed. (Think of the person who returns to society after leaving Plato's cave. The returnee will be ridiculed by the citizens of the cave. See Chapter 7 — The Journey Upward.) Should Citizen A merely adhere to the wishes of the majority?

In his famous essay on "Civil Disobedience," Thoreau tackles questions similar to those above. "Unjust laws exist: shall we be content to obey them, or shall we endeavor to amend them, and obey them until we have succeeded or shall we transgress them at once?"[1] If you "endeavor to amend" the laws, but obey them until they can be exchanged for just ones, are you not, in the meantime, acting immorally? According to Thoreau, if the injustice "...is of such a nature that it requires you to be the agent of injustice to another, then, I say, break the law?"[2]

In an essay entitled "Slavery in Massachusetts," Thoreau uses the institution of slavery as an example of an unjust system that requires correcting.[3] While one may work tirelessly to pass anti-slavery laws, innocent people are being deprived of their basic rights and are being abused in countless ways. Slave families continue to be broken up at the whim of the slave owner.

How can slavery be tolerated for even a moment? John Brown attempted to start a violent slave insurrection. Thoreau was unwilling to condemn Brown. In a speech entitled "A Plea for Captain John Brown," Thoreau wrote:

> The slave-ship is on her way, crowded with its dying victims ... a
> small crew of slaveholders ... is smothering four millions under the
> hatches, and yet the politician asserts that the only proper way by which
> deliverance is to be obtained, is by "the quiet diffusion of the sentiments
> of humanity," without any "outbreak."[4]

Suppose violence is not considered an option in the attempt to
replace unjust laws with just ones. The second movie in this chapter provides a wonderful reenactment of the life of the chief proponent of non-
violent civil disobedience — Gandhi. Turn now, however, to the first
movie, *Gattaca*.

Movie 26: *Gattaca*

Director: Andrew Niccol; 1 hour, 46 minutes; 1997
Watch the movie.

Questions to ponder:

1. The "special features" of the "Gattaca" DVD contain a series of
"lost scenes" that did not make the final cut. One is a coda. In part, the
coda says,

> "We have now evolved to the point where we can direct our own evo-
> lution. Had we acquired the knowledge sooner, the following people
> may never have been born:
>
>> Abraham Lincoln — Marfan Syndrome
>> Emily Dickinson — Manic Depression
>> Vincent Van Gogh — Epilepsy
>> Albert Einstein — Dyslexia
>> John F. Kennedy — Addison's Disease
>> Rita Hayworth — Alzheimer's Disease
>> Ray Charles — Primary Glaucoma
>> Stephen Hawking — Amyotrophic Lateral Sclerosis
>> Jackie Joyner-Kersee — Asthma
>
> Of course, the other birth that may never have taken place is your
> own.

All of the above persons, including yourself, would be classed as "de-
gene-erates" in the society portrayed in the film. Is the world better off
with the above persons in it or with genetically programmed human
beings who approach physical and intellectual perfection?

Jerome Morrow (Ethan Hawke) leads Irene (Uma Thurman) to the blood-sampling entrance of the Gattaca Corporation in *Gattaca* (1997).

2. Were you cheering Vincent (Ethan Hawke) on? Did you hope he would be successful and get on the flight to Titan? Were you wrong to have such an attitude? After all, he had a serious heart condition. He couldn't even ride an exercise machine without his heart acting up. Do you really want Vincent being part of a hugely expensive expedition to Titan? What turmoil would occur on that expedition if Vincent's heart gave out? Suppose he wanted to be a jet pilot. Would you want to be a passenger on a plane piloted by him? If not, shouldn't you change your view and hope he fails in his quest to make it to Titan? Why or why not?

3. Vincent and Irene (Uma Thurman) love each other. In the film, they make love. Suppose she gets pregnant and has a "God-child"—a child who is not genetically engineered and who will have many imperfections. Are Vincent and Irene being selfish by bringing a child into a world in which the best jobs are only for those who approach physical perfection? Are *we* selfish by bringing into the world children who will suffer from various imperfections?

4. Jerome (Jude Law) tried to commit suicide by stepping in front of a car. He did it because he came in second place in a race and he felt

like a failure. Vincent's brother, Anton (Loren Dean), can't stand to be beaten at swimming by Vincent. Does that indicate that almost perfect human beings will experience mental suffering when they fail to reach goals?

5. I placed *Gattaca* in a chapter on civil disobedience. A society that does not allow a "de-gene-erate" to strive for greatness seems to be an unjust society. One feels Vincent has a right to be disobedient and break that society's rules. He is engaged in fraudulent behavior, but the fraud is necessary so he can rise to the heights of personal achievement. Does he go too far at any time (for example, when he beats the policeman who tries to stop him outside the concert hall)? Vincent did not kill the Mission Director, but suppose he had because the Director found out Vincent was a de-gene-erate. Would Vincent have gone too far then?

6. Why did Lamar (Xander Berkeley) ignore the fact that Vincent is an "invalid"? Apparently, he knew that fact early on because he noticed Vincent used the wrong hand when giving a urine sample.

7. What evidence is there that humankind is on a path towards something like the life projected in *Gattaca*?

Another excellent movie that offers numerous examples of where society is probably heading, and the future loss of various freedoms, is *Minority Report* (2002).

Movie 27: *Gandhi*

Director: Richard Attenborough; 3 hours, 10 minutes; 1982

As you watch this movie, you will forget it is Ben Kingsley on the screen. You will believe you are witnessing Gandhi and the central events of his life. Many scenes in the film are almost indistinguishable from actual news footage and still photographs. You can verify the authenticity of many scenes by checking the special feature on the DVD that contains news clips.

Watch the movie.

Questions to ponder:

1. In the film, Gandhi claims, "There is no people on earth who would not prefer their own bad government to the good government of an alien power." (He specifically is making the point that Indians prefer

Margaret Bourke-White (Candice Bergen) photographs Gandhi (Ben Kingsley).

that the British give up control of India.) Do you think there are exceptions to Gandhi's claim? Under what conditions would you prefer an alien government over a bad government made up of "your people"?

2. Gandhi claimed that "happiness does not come from things, even 20th century things. It can come from work and pride in what you do." Can *you* imagine being happy without working or having pride in what you do?

3. Gandhi consistently stressed non-violent action. In the film, Margaret Bourke-White (Candice Bergen) asks him, "Do you really believe you could use non-violence against someone like Hitler?" Gandhi's answer is "yes," but he admits there would be a great amount of suffering before a peaceful state were achieved. Do you think non-violence will always lead to the desired result? Gandhi was successful in getting the British to relinquish their power in India. Martin Luther King, Jr., brought about a great deal of worthwhile change by using non-violence. What kinds of harmful social conditions, if any, do you think could not be eliminated by non-violence?

AN ADDITIONAL RECOMMENDATION FOR CIVIL DISOBEDIENCE

Bread and Roses (2000). Adrien Brody in a pre–*Pianist* role (see Movie 47). Based on a true story that centers on a movement to guarantee just treatment of immigrant workers in Los Angeles. A similar theme is explored in *Norma Rae* (1979). The latter film, starring Sally Field, deals with an attempt to organize 800 workers in a textile factory.

9

Death

In the movies of this chapter, the topic is death. In Chapter 16, love will be stressed. Are there any other themes in cinema more common than love and death? Look over the list of films covered earlier in the book. Think of the dominant presence of love and/or death in the majority of them: sending a man to his death in *12 Angry Men*; the love of another man's wife by an imposter (*The Return of Martin Guerre*); murder in *Rashomon*; being surrounded by death and facing death in *Abandon Ship*; the love of a field in *The Field*; fulfilling one's duty to the beloved deceased husband (*The Road Home*); the love and compassion of Jesus and Buddha (*The Last Temptation of Christ* and *Little Buddha*); and so on.

Most movies, however, will not center on the issue of death to the degree you will find in the seven films covered in this chapter. It may seem that the may be morbid, but in viewing them you will find many moments that are also uplifting.

Movie 28: *Shadowlands*

Director: Richard Attenborough; 2 hours, 13 minutes; 1993

Shadowlands is a wonderful retelling of a crucial portion of the life of the great Christian thinker and author, C.S. Lewis. *After* watching the movie, I strongly recommend you read his short book *A Grief Observed*.

Near the beginning of the film, Lewis (Anthony Hopkins) lectures on the traditionally important religious dilemma called the "problem of evil." Lewis asks where God was when a bus drove into a group of marine cadets, killing 24. Why didn't God stop the bus? If God is good, he would want to stop the bus. If God is all-powerful, he *could* stop the bus. If God is all-knowing, he would know the bus accident would kill some of the cadets. Since He didn't stop the accident from happening, it seems He must be either (a) not all-good or (b) not all-powerful or (c) not all-knowing.

Anthony Hopkins as the Christian philosopher C.S. Lewis, and Debra Winger as Joy, the love of Lewis' life in *Shadowlands* (1993).

I used to think the "problem of evil" was a pseudo-problem. However, it now seems to me that *any* attempt to resolve the problem involves the re-emergence of the problem under another guise. If, for example, you say God allowed the cadets to be killed in order to test the faith of surviving friends and relatives, a serious question of justice arises. If I torture Person A to test Person B, I've clearly done something evil. How would *you* respond to the problem of evil?

The problem of evil holds a critical place in *Shadowlands*. As the plot unfolds, you will see why it was introduced at the beginning of the movie.

Watch the movie.

Questions to ponder:

1. Several times the point is made that God wants us to "grow up." Suffering is what leads us out of the nursery. The child chooses "safety"; the adult chooses suffering. Do you agree with this view? Why or why not?

2. Joy (Debra Winger) makes a very important statement on the wonderful trip to the valley in Herefordshire: "The pain then is part of

the happiness now." What does she mean? Why is it so important to her that Lewis see the truth of that statement?

Movie 29: *Under the Sand*

Director: Francois Ozon; 1 hour, 35 minutes; 2000
Watch the movie.

A question to ponder:

1. The first time I watched *Under the Sand* I was certain Jean (Bruno Cremer) had merely drowned. I saw Marie (Charlotte Rampling) and Jean as happily married. The fact that Jean's mother said he was "bored" with Marie and "wanted a new life" seemed to me to be the judgment of a mother who could not face the possibility that her son was dead. I saw many things during my second viewing I missed the first time around. *Every* sequence that centered on Jean at the beginning of the film shows an unhappy man. Look at those scenes again. At the rest stop, and during the first moments at the summer house, he is pensive. While picking up kindling for the fireplace he seems depressed. Before dinner he is deep in thought, staring at a wine bottle. While Marie sits in a chair, he looks at her and doesn't speak. The look is not a look of love. In bed, Marie hugs him. There is no response from Jean. Only Marie is happy. She seems oblivious to his state of mind. Jean chooses a beach that doesn't get crowded. Why? So he can sneak off without anyone seeing him? So he can drown himself without being seen? At the beach he asks her if she wants to swim. She says no. He looks at her — a blank look. He looks at the waves. What must he be thinking? And then he is gone. Do you think Jean (a) deserted Marie and is

Charlotte Rampling looks out to sea in *Under the Sand* (2000).

living somewhere far away, (b) accidentally drowned, or (c) committed suicide by drowning himself? What evidence do you give for your conclusion?

My interpretation: Given the results of the genetic tests on the body that was found, and the dental records that showed a match, as well as the fact that the swimming trunks and watch fit Marie's original description, it seems highly probable it was Jean's body that was found. Marie couldn't accept the truth, however, and denied that the watch belonged to Jean. Because of his previous behavior, and because of the fact that he had prescriptions for dealing with depression, it seems likely that Jean committed suicide.

Movie 30: *Fearless*

Director: Peter Weir; 2 hours, 2 minutes; 1993

In 1927, Martin Heidegger's *Being and Time* was published, stunning many in the world of philosophy. *Being and Time* contains a wonderfully systematic presentation of existential themes, themes such as those discussed in Chapter 4 (Anxiety and Inauthenticity). One section in particular stirred a great deal of controversy: a section on the human individual's "being-towards-death." Heidegger's main ideas in that section are as follows: "Death" is defined as "the possibility of no-longer-being-able-to-be-there."[1] That possibility is so terrifying that every individual runs from accepting the fact that he or she is going to die. Human beings project future otherworldly lives after death and cover up the possibility of their future nonexistence by engaging in meaningless recreation. Human beings thus miss an authentic relation with the people and places and things of their present lives. In fact, by denying future death and present "being-towards-death," human beings lose their individuality. By overcoming the "tranquilization" that arises in denying death, a person becomes aware of their existential anxiety. According to Heidegger, "anxiety individualizes."[2] Someone who runs from their impending death will hide in the crowd, and then the individual will be "covered up." Once a person has achieved a "freedom towards death," he or she has replaced the tranquilized state with a more authentic being towards the world.

Fearless raises issues found in *Being and Time*. Are we authentically accepting our own finitude? Are we in an authentic relationship with

Jeff Bridges in *Fearless* (1993).

other people and with things of this world, or are we letting life pass us by?

Watch the movie.

Questions to ponder:

1. What could possibly account for the extreme change in Max Klein (Jeff Bridges)? One moment in the airplane he is terrified, and the next he is in a state of peace. From being out of control, he takes control, calms other passengers, and, after the plane crashes, saves a number of lives.

2. After his character change in the airplane, is Max sane or crazy? What is the significance of his asking his wife Laura (Isabella Rossellini) to "save" him?

3. Carla Rodrigo (Rosie Perez) says to Max that God had hurt her forever. However, she still believes in God. Max answers that, "People don't so much believe in God as they choose not to believe in nothing." Is Max saying something similar to what Heidegger says about the tranquilization undergone by people who are faced with future nothingness (death)? Does Max have an "authentic-being-toward-death?" Does Carla achieve that authentic attitude?

4. At one point, Carla indicates she believes there is no meaning in life if there is not life after death. I have heard many students express the same sentiment. It seems Max responds to this idea when he unplugs the video game his son and a friend are playing. He is turning his son away from shallow video games to things much more meaningful. After he "died" in the airplane crash, he savored those valuable things he had taken for granted. Life is good when you taste a strawberry, tell the truth, or help those in need. I agree with Max. People who fail to see meaning in life without life after death should look again. Seeing a child smile, reading a great novel, hiking in the Grand Canyon, breaking your best golf score, watching the movies covered in this book — how could life after death top such things? What is your view on this matter?

Movie 31: *Whose Life Is It Anyway?*

Director: John Badham; 1 hour, 59 minutes; 1981

Whose Life Is It Anyway? is a movie about euthanasia. A philosophical distinction must be made between "active euthanasia" and "passive euthanasia." "Active euthanasia" occurs when someone (usually a medical professional) actively does something that will lead to the death of a sufferer who has no reasonable hope of recovery. "Passive euthanasia," on the other hand, occurs when procedures that would keep the sufferer alive are not utilized. It is the latter that is the central issue brought forth in this film.

A person can choose from several options when he/she decides whether to support euthanasia or not. For example: (A) One may be opposed to both active and passive euthanasia. (B) One may be opposed to active euthanasia but support passive euthanasia (generally, a person who chooses this option would accept the position that simply "letting someone die" is not murder, whereas active euthanasia is). (C) One may support active euthanasia and be opposed to passive euthanasia. Passive euthanasia, it is argued, is a cruel, unnecessary prolonging of suffering. Active euthanasia shows compassion for the sufferer.

Watch the movie.

Questions to ponder:

1. The jacket of the video asks a very important question. Dr. Emerson (John Cassavetes) prolonged the life of Ken Harrison (Richard Drey-

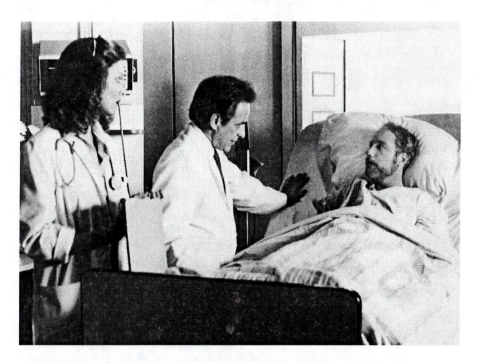

Richard Dreyfuss (right) stars as a sculptor who displays exceptional courage and wit. Christine Lahti and John Cassavetes appear as his doctors in *Whose Life Is It, Anyway?* (1981).

fuss). The question is: "For what purpose?" Do you have an answer to that question?

2. Ken says to Pat (Janet Eilber), "Do you know that every time you walk into the room you remind me of the way things were? Every time I look at you I see what I cannot do and what I will never do again. And I can't stand it!" He wants her to leave and not come back. What should Pat do? At the moment he says those words, does Ken love Pat? Does he hate her?

3. What would utilitarians say about whether Ken should be released from the hospital? Remember — other than Pat — Ken has no living relatives.

4. Ken says that physicians seem to think that keeping a patient alive is all that matters. Ken believes physicians should also be concerned about the *quality* of life. What do you think?

5. Dr. Emerson holds that Ken is in a state of depression and is not fit to make decisions concerning his welfare. In the future, Ken may over-

come his depressed state and be glad he is alive. Might Dr. Emerson be correct?

6. Most case studies involving euthanasia concern patients who are in great physical pain and who are going to die in the not-so-distant future. In *Whose Life Is It Anyway?* the scenario is different. Without passive euthanasia Ken Harrison very probably would continue to live a long time. Do you think that euthanasia is more acceptable if the person being euthanized were experiencing physical pain that is intense and enduring rather than if he or she were in Ken's situation?

7. Many opponents of any form of euthanasia claim that if one accepts euthanasia, there is no telling where things will stop. Will Alzheimer's patients be next? Political "undesirables?" Do you think there are such dangers?

Movie 32: *Dead Man Walking*

Director: Tim Robbins; 2 hours, 2 minutes; 1995
Warning: *Dead Man Walking* contains some very disturbing violent scenes.
Watch the movie.

Questions to ponder:

1. Many supporters of capital punishment argue that it acts as a deterrent. Do you think capital punishment is a deterrent?

2. A common objection to capital punishment is that many persons who commit capital crimes are not in control of themselves when they commit the crime. They are not acting out of free will and thus are not responsible for their actions. In many cases, it may *seem* that the "criminal" is responsible, but he or she may have a serious mental disorder that just cannot be detected. Thus, it is too easy to punish someone who, instead, should be the recipient of medical treatment. Compassion should be shown to such a person. Do you think capital punishment should be eliminated because of the possibility of such a mistake? Was Matthew Poncelet (Sean Penn) responsible for the crimes for which he was convicted? (Think of his background and his claim that he used drugs the night of the murder.) What about the possibility that even if there is no reasonable doubt that X is guilty, X *might* be innocent, and thus killing

Sister Helen Prejean (Susan Sarandon) shows compassion to inmate Matthew Poncelet (Sean Penn) in *Dead Man Walking* (1995).

X is itself a case of murder. "X is guilty" is a synthetic judgment! Remember the plot of *12 Angry Men* (Movie 1).

3. Another criticism of capital punishment is that wealthy and influential people can afford better lawyers than those who are poor. As Matthew Poncelet says in the movie, "Ain't nobody with money on death row." Also, elements of racism still permeate our society and thus can taint our juries. If this is the case, those charged with capital crimes may not be treated equitably. Matthew Poncelet has the cards stacked against him because of his low social status. Is such inequity sufficient reason to eliminate capital punishment? (In the movie we discover that Matthew received a death sentence and his partner received life imprisonment because the latter "had a better lawyer." Matthew just had "bad luck" with the lawyer he was granted.)

4. Which do you think others a better portrayal of a murderer and his execution — *Dead Man Walking* or *The Decalogue, Part V* (Movie 20)? Which — if either — do you think presents a better case for abolishing capital punishment? Or have these two movies reinforced your belief that capital punishment is justified?

Movie 33: *Resurrection*

Director: Daniel Petrie; 1 hour, 42 minutes; 2000

"Is there life after death?" is a question that intrigues many people, philosophers included. At his trial, Socrates held that it is the goal of the philosopher to prepare for death. People who aren't wise have an irrational fear of death. A good, rational person, however, has no such fear. For one of the great works of philosophy, read Plato's *Apology*—his account of Socrates' trial. It is a short but wonderful read.

Plato created a series of famous proofs for life after death. These proofs can be found in his dialogue, *Phaedo*. *Phaedo* recounts the execution of Socrates. Plato's proofs are placed in the mouth of Socrates, though Socrates probably never uttered them. The major step in one of the proofs centers on the idea that we have knowledge about perfect things and perfect reality. That knowledge could not have been obtained from our life here on earth, because nothing on earth is perfect. Therefore, this knowledge would have had to have been obtained in a previous life utterly different from this spatio-tempored realm. If Plato is correct, a person's soul existed in a more real, more perfect world before existing in the present one. If our souls exist in a perfect world before we are born, then there is reason to think that when the body dies, a person's soul will return to that world.

Most believers in life after death, including Plato, are "dualists." A dualist believes that here on earth humans are made up of two utterly different "substances": mental substance (the soul) and physical substance (the body). At death, it is the body that dies. The death of the body means that the parts of the body break down and decay. The soul, however, is not made up of physical parts and so cannot break down. It follows that the soul cannot die.

Philosophers who are critical of the concept of life after death tend to be critical of "dualism." It is argued that dualism is false because it leads to what is known as the "mind/body problem." If the mind (soul) and body are two substances, and they have nothing in common, then there is no way to see how they could possibly interact. (If they have something in common, then it would seem the death of one would involve the death of the other.)

Philosophers also tend to be very skeptical about claims of "near-death experiences" like the one depicted in *Resurrection*. Sentences like,

"I died and saw loved ones who had previously died," and, "I died and saw a white light that was the light of heaven," are synthetic sentences and could be false. Did the person who had the near-death experience really die? Did the person really "see" dead loved ones or did he/she merely *think* he/she saw them? How can it be known that the white light is coming from heaven? Maybe the light is from the fires of hell and the devil

Ellen Burstyn performs a miracle in *Resurrection* (2000).

is merely playing tricks on the person near death. Basically, nothing logically follows from "I saw a white light" except "I saw a white light."

Concerning the faith-healing scenes in the movie, philosophers would tend to say what Cal Carpenter (Sam Shepard) says in the movie: "You know, I got a theory about all this healing.... My theory is that them that's cured is got the sickness in their mind and then somebody comes along and prays over them and if they believe that person can make them well — well, then they're cured." Is it not the case that if they go to a psychiatrist they might be cured also?

My view is that people who readily accept other's testimonies about near-death experiences are extremely gullible people. In my introductory philosophy classes I sometimes claim I have come across an amazing book that explains how to accomplish seemingly impossible feats. For example, I claim I have learned how to read people's minds. I tell my students I will leave the room. While I am gone each student is to point at other students in the room until, by some group dynamic, everyone points at one person. I am then brought back into the room. After I think really hard for a bit, I tell which student was pointed at. I explain that, "I felt vibes and could hear voices. The voices were coming from the students' minds directing me to the person they pointed at." How did I do it? Some students use their background in psychology to postulate it was body language that gave away the answer. However, I convince a substantial number that I indeed have this special mystical knack. The problem: It was too easy to fool these intelligent students. (How much easier it would be to fool people less trained to be critical thinkers.) The explanation of my wonderful ability? Before class I take a student aside. That student, with a mere twitch of a finger when I stand next to the targeted student, tells me what I want to know. It is that simple to get students to believe some supernatural event has just occurred. If I — an amateur — can dupe people into thinking I have extraordinary abilities, isn't it reasonable to think other people are gullibly accepting "near-death experiences" as "*after-death experiences*," and gullibly accepting faith healing as having supernatural roots?

Watch the movie.

Questions to ponder:

1. David Hume wrote: "A wise man proportions his belief to the evidence."[3] Do you agree with that quote? Why or why not? Then: Do

you think there is sufficient evidence to merit belief in claims of near-death experiences like the one made in *Resurrection*? Is there sufficient evidence to justify believing faith-healing claims like those portrayed in *Resurrection*? What *would* be sufficient evidence to justify one's belief in such claims?

Movie 34: *The Seventh Seal*

Director: Ingmar Bergman; 1 hour, 36 minutes; 1957

The Seventh Seal is a masterpiece filled with unforgettable images and characters. Notice, for example, Antonius Block (Max von Sydow) putting Death (Bengt Ekerot) off for a bit by challenging him to a game of chess. Notice also Antonius sharing a meal of wild strawberries and milk supplied by the traveling actors — husband and wife Joseph (Nils Poppe) and Mary (Bibi Andersson). There is the behavior of people surrounded by the Black Plague, and the compassion shown by Antonius and his squire, Jons (Gunnar Bjornstrand), though the latter also possesses a cutting cynical edge.

You'll have to ask yourself what the movie "means." Clearly, Antonius is searching for God, and thus the film could have been included in Chapter 6 (as it deals with religious issues). Bergman made this film at the height of the existentialist movement, and the existential themes of the film would fit well in Chapter 4 (Anxiety and Inauthenticity). I placed *The Seventh Seal* in the current chapter on death because Death is an ever-present force in the movie.

In the middle of the 14th century, Antonius is returning to his native Sweden from the Crusades. What he faces is a land filled with death caused by the Black Plague. Bergman, however, was not referring to the Medieval Period — he was expressing what people of the 1950s were facing (or, since *The Seventh Seal* is timeless, what *we* are facing in the 21st century). The war against Hitler, Mussolini and Hirohito was won. But now a new plague was on the loose — the possibility of nuclear annihilation. (In 1963, von Sydow and Bjornstrand were brought together again by Bergman in a film called *Winter Light*, in which the terror of possible nuclear catastrophe must be faced.)

Existentialists stress the absurdity of religious belief, the death of God (or the "eclipse of God"), and the angst one must face because of one's impending death. For existentialists, belief is an inadequate foun-

Bengt Ekerot as Death in Ingmar Bergman's *The Seventh Seal* (1957).

dation for human life. What is needed is *knowledge*. Antonius tries to communicate with God, saying, "We're small and afraid and without knowledge." He wants to *see* God. He can't believe in something he doesn't see. He needs to feel there is some meaning to his life, a life in which Death is tapping him on the shoulder. (At one point, expressing the meaninglessness of his life, Antonius says he is in "boring company" — he is in company with himself.)

All of the above religious, cultural and existential themes are at work in *The Seventh Seal.*

Watch the movie.

Questions to ponder:

1. "Death" is often portrayed as a person. Why is this done? Death isn't really a person. Or is He/She?

2. After Death wins the chess match, he asks Antonius, "Did you gain by the delay?" Antonius answers, "Yes." *What* did he gain? Earlier he said he wanted to do something meaningful before he dies. He does something meaningful. What is it?

3. If you have viewed *Hannah and Her Sisters* (Movie 9) and read my questions/comments on that film, you know that the scene in which the Woody Allen character stumbles into a Marx Brothers movie is filled with meaning. I think the scene in which Antonius has a simple meal with Mary and Joseph is filled with the same type of meaning. What do *you* think is the significance of that scene? (Important: as Antonius leaves the meal he again encounters Death. But Antonius now seems at peace.)

4. Jons calls us to "feel, to the very end, the triumph of being alive." If one could experience such triumph — to the very end — would one be "cheating" Death?

Other "must see" movies by Ingmar Bergman:

Wild Strawberries (1957)
Persona (1966)
Cries and Whispers (1972)
Fanny and Alexander (1984)

ADDITIONAL RECOMMENDATIONS ON THE THEME OF DEATH

The Son's Room (2001). Deservedly won the Palme d'Or at Cannes. Nanni Moretti directed the film and is unforgettable as Giovanni, a psychoanalyst who faces what every parent dreads.

In the Bedroom (2001). *The Son's Room* listed above was also released in 2001. Because of the general American prejudice against foreign films, few saw *The Son's Room*. Many saw *In the Bedroom*. I believe that most people who view both movies will grant that the acting and power of *The Son's Room* win out over *In the Bedroom*.

The Sweet Hereafter (1997). When a tragedy occurs, people seek to discover who was to blame. Some who are not responsible may feel guilt. *The Sweet Hereafter* investigates the lives of those who endure the trauma of the accidental death of loved ones.

Ordinary People (1980). Robert Redford's directional debut. Watching *The Son's Room*, *In the Bedroom*, *The Sweet Hereafter* and *Ordinary People* on consecutive evenings would provide much to talk about. Comparing these movies that are so similar in some respects, yet so different in others, would constitute a wonderful intellectual adventure.

Ghost (1990). You will not find many philosophers who believe there are such things as ghosts. Still, only the most cold-hearted will fail to be moved by the romantic line of *Ghost*. There is chemistry between Demi Moore and Patrick Swayze. Whoopi Goldberg won a Best Supporting Actress Oscar for her role as a hokey psychic. I find Whoopi's character to be corny and distracting.

My Life as a Dog (1997). If I had to list my "most unforgettable" characters in movies, near the top would be Ingemar (Anton Glanzelius), the 12-year-old central character of *My Life as a Dog*. The director is Lasse Hallstrom, who also helmed the very popular *Chocolat* (2001).

Terms of Endearment (1983). From the novel by Larry McMurtry, who also wrote *Lonesome Dove*. Shirley MacLaine won an Oscar for Best Actress. Debra Winger's performance as Shirley's daughter deserved more notice than it received. Compare her performance here with that in *Shadowlands* (Movie 28). They are, at times, almost indistinguishable. Although Jack Nicholson's portrayal of a retired astronaut earned him an Oscar for Best Supporting Actor, I don't find his contribution to be all that noteworthy.

What Dreams May Come (1998). *What Dreams May Come* borders on fantasy, à la *Ghost*. The DVD contains an interesting alternate ending. Oscar-winning visual effects stand out. Max von Sydow appears in the film. It is interesting to compare his role here with that in *The Seventh Seal* (Movie 34).

Autumn Spring (2001). A more accurate translation of the Czech title is *Indian Summer*. The three main stars (Vlastimil Brodsky as Fanda, Stanislav Zindulka as Eda, and Stella Zazvorkova as Emilie) shine. It is so refreshing seeing such grand performances from elderly actors. Who needs handsome young 'uns in movies when there are performances like these? There is something perhaps you should not know before viewing this film. Maybe it would be best not to know it *after* viewing it! But — now that I've mentioned it, if you must know — watch the movie and *then* read the following sentence, the letters of which are written in reverse order: *.2002 ni edicius dettimmoc (adnaF) yksdorB limitsalV*

Though admittedly hokey, I simply don't want your reaction to the movie to be colored by this information.

10

War

I can find tremendous drama in movies that contain little action. Think of *Casablanca.* Think of *My Dinner with Andre.* But good war movies have a dramatic impact that, perhaps, is unmatched. A question to ponder: *Why* do good war movies affect the viewer so much? After all, most audience members have never been in a war.

Well over 50 million people died as a result of war in the 20th century. Start counting to 50 million. Each number stands for a human being: 1, 2, 3, 4, 5, 6, 7 ... are you getting close? Think of the suffering of the loved ones who survived. Numbers, however, do not tell anything about what it feels to be the civilians caught in a war zone, or anything about the destruction of cities. Numbers do not convey the stench of death. The old saying "war is hell" is true, but again, people who have not experienced war firsthand can not truly know what that hell is like.

Visit Verdun in France. Except for trees that have since grown, the battleground has remained largely untouched by the French, who hold it to be sacred ground. Hundreds of thousands died there — the area earned the nickname the "Mincing Machine." Visit the American cemetery overlooking Omaha Beach in Normandy. There lie rows and rows of Americans who died so far from home. The dramatic story of Pickett's Charge at Gettysburg has been told and retold. But what was it like to be a Confederate soldier crossing a mile of fields to devastating defeat? In war, two groups of human beings, both believing God is on their side, both hating the other, are engaged in a death struggle. Why?

There follows one film about the Civil War (*The Red Badge of Courage*), one about World War I (*Paths of Glory*), one on World War II (*Saving Private Ryan*), one on Vietnam (*Full Metal Jacket*) and one on the Balkan War (*No Man's Land*).

A scene from John Huston's *The Red Badge of Courage* (1951), starring Audie Murphy (left). On the right is Bill Mauldin.

Movie 35: *The Red Badge of Courage*

Director: John Huston; 1 hour, 10 minutes; 1951

I recommend reading Stephen Crane's *The Red Badge of Courage* before watching the film. John Huston directed the picture and did an excellent job conveying almost all of the major events covered in the novel. Audie Murphy, who plays the young soldier Henry Fleming, is a pleasure to watch.

Watch the movie.

Questions to ponder:

1. Wilson (Bill Maudlin) has a premonition that he won't survive the day. There are a number of verified reports from the Civil War era of soldiers on both sides who had such premonitions and who indeed died. Do you think there is anything to such premonitions? Remember: Wilson does *not* die.

2. The novel and the film both effectively portray the fear of being

a coward in battle and the stigma attached to that label. Some "cowards" were shot as examples to other soldiers of what would happen if they did not do their duty. The following questions would also fit well into Chapter 5 (Fate and Determinism): Is a person responsible for being a coward and running away from danger in war? Is being a coward or being brave something one can control? Would anyone really *choose* to be a "coward"?

3. In most war movies, war novels, and, indeed, factual accounts of soldier life in war, there is a clear-cut distinction between the mindsets of "greenhorns" and "veterans." What kind of generalizations would you make about those two differing mindsets? (The novel *The Red Badge of Courage* does a fairly good job of showing the difference between Wilson as a greenhorn and Wilson as a battle-tested veteran.)

Movie 36: *Paths of Glory*

Director: Stanley Kubrick; 1 hour, 27 minutes; 1957

I recommend reading Humphrey Cobb's novel *Paths of Glory* before viewing the film. The drama of the novel is even greater than that of the movie. The characters in the novel are clearly French — as they should be. Of the film, one critic has written that the "illusion of reality is blown completely whenever anybody talks."[1] Kirk Douglas as a World War I French colonel? Wait until you experience Emile Meyer as a French priest. However, in spite of serious miscasting, Kubrick's early film still packs a wallop.

Watch the movie.

Questions to ponder:

1. Why were the men executed? After all, they were not cowards.

2. Is there anything Colonel Dax (Kirk Douglas) had left undone in his efforts to save the three men? Think about when he was ordered by General Mireau (George Macready) to lead an obviously futile attack against the Ant Hill? Did he do all he should have done to get that attack canceled?

Additional comments:

Paths of Glory may seem to have an unrealistic plot. However, the futile attack portrayed in the film and the unbelievable execution of three

Stanley Kubrick's World War I drama *Paths of Glory* (1957), starring Kirk Douglas (right). Supporting actor Wayne Morris appears on the left.

soldiers is based on fact. For an excellent background on the stalemate of World War I trench warfare, the execution by lottery of soldiers to be used as examples, and the massive mutiny that shook the incompetent French military leadership in 1917, read *Dare Call It Treason* by Richard M. Watt (New York: Simon and Schuster, 1963).

Paths of Glory is one of a series of films and novels that scathingly attack the absurdity that was World War I, and call into question all warfare. Erich Maria Remarque's 1929 novel *All Quiet on the Western Front*, and the film of the same name (1930), are heartily recommended. Three other powerful books in the same vein:

Under Fire— Henri Barbusse (1917)
Men in War— Adolf Andreas Latzko (1918)
Johnny Got His Gun— Dalton Trumbo (1939)

Movie 37: *Saving Private Ryan*

Director: Steven Spielberg; 2 hours, 49 minutes; 1999

Is Spielberg's film of the D-Day assault on the Normandy beaches as realistic as possible a representation of what it is like to be in battle? It seems to be, but only those who were there can tell for sure. The viewer, of course, is not nauseated and scared to death as were the troops in the landing boats. The viewer is not surrounded by death as were those trapped on the beach.

A scene from Steven Spielberg's *Saving Private Ryan* (1999), starring Tom Hanks (left), Matt Damon (middle) and Edward Burns (right).

After the harrowing landing sequences, the film turns to a post-beach plot. But is that story as realistic as what came before, or is it merely another Hollywood cop-out? Captain Miller (Tom Hanks) and a bunch of soldiers go on an impossible quest. So what? Quest plots bring up important issues about duty, comradeship, and courage. (Think of *The Lord of the Rings*.) For me, whether the quest in *Saving Private Ryan* could be brought to a successful conclusion is not as important as the fact that many real-life American soldiers would have tried. To save Private Ryan, they would have put their lives on the line.

Watch the movie.

Questions to ponder:

1. Captain Miller says, "This Ryan better be worth it. He better go home, cure some disease or invent the longest lasting light bulb or something." As he is dying, Captain Miller says to Private Ryan (Matt Damon): "Earn this." Should Captain Miller *care* about how Ryan will turn out? Think of what Kant said (see Chapter 3 — Doing One's Duty) about the consequences of one's moral decisions being of no importance. What is crucial is doing one's duty.

2. Would a utilitarian (see Chapter 2 — The Greatest Happiness Principle) support endangering eight lives to save one? If yes, on what grounds?

3. Captain Miller ordered the German prisoner to head to the Allied lines and turn himself in as a POW. Others in Miller's squad wanted the German killed. Since the German turns up later at the fighting for the bridge and kills at least one American, would it have been better to have killed him? Corporal Upham (Jeremy Davies) had argued that the German's life should be spared, but at the bridge, after capturing the German, he kills him. At the time Upham kills him, the German was a POW. If he should not have been shot the first time he was captured because POWs have rights, then doesn't it follow he should not have been killed when he again became a prisoner of the squad?

Movie 38: *Full Metal Jacket*

Director: Stanley Kubrick; 1 hour, 56 minutes; 1987

There is not much plot to *Full Metal Jacket*. The film consists of two clearly separate episodes. One episode captures the trials and tribulations

Dorian Harewood in Stanley Kubrick's *Full Metal Jacket* (1987).

of Marine recruits going through basic training on Parris Island. The other follows Private Joker's (Matthew Modine) experiences after he completes basic training and becomes a journalist for *Stars and Stripes* in Vietnam. The latter episode particularly stresses what happens when Private Joker is drawn into the fighting during the Tet Offensive.

What there is in *Full Metal Jacket* is Stanley Kubrick's dynamic direction and the memorable acting of Modine and Lee Ermey. The latter plays a hard-driven drill instructor, Gunnery Sergeant Hartman.

Watch the movie.

Questions to ponder:

1. Joker, reporting for *Stars and Stripes*, is ordered by his superior to falsify the account of a skirmish by adding the detail that an enemy soldier was killed. He is also ordered to use the words "sweep and clear" instead of "search and destroy." Such manipulative reporting of what was

occurring in Vietnam certainly was common. When America is at war, should American citizens accept such journalistic practices as necessary for the greater good?

2. Joker wears a peace symbol. On his helmet he writes "Born to Kill." When people wear symbols or a slogan they are expressing something. What is Joker expressing with the peace symbol and the message on his helmet?

3. *Full Metal Jacket* explores the dehumanization of both traditional Parris Island basic training and combat action. In addition, Joker, as well as major characters in numerous other war movies, experiences a loss of innocence. What is lost when a human being becomes "dehumanized" or "loses innocence" as portrayed in *Full Metal Jacket*? How is a "humanized, innocent" human being different from one who is "dehumanized" and who has lost innocence? Is it good for military personnel to become "dehumanized?"

Two of the films in this chapter were directed by Stanley Kubrick. Other films by this master director:

Spartacus (1960)

Lolita (1962)

Dr. Strangelove or: How I Learned to Stop Worrying and Love the Bomb (1964). Scary, because *Dr. Strangelove* begins to make you feel that our military leaders may indeed act like Group Captain Lionel Mandrake (Peter Sellers), General Jack D. Ripper (Sterling Hayden), President Merkin Muffley (Sellers again), Dr. Strangelove (Sellers again), and General Buck Turgidson (George C. Scott).

2001: A Space Odyssey (1968). One of the great science fiction films.

A Clockwork Orange (1972). Warning: Very difficult to watch. Extreme violence!

Barry Lyndon (1975)

The Shining (1980). One of the great horror films.

Eyes Wide Shut (1999). Warning: Sexually explicit scenes.

Two excellent books on Stanley Kubrick's work are *Stanley Kubrick: 7 Films Analyzed* by Randy Rasmussen (Jefferson, North Carolina: McFarland, 2001) and *Stanley Kubrick, Director: A Visual Analysis* by Alexander Walker, Ulrich Ruchti and Sybil Taylor (New York: W.W. Norton, 2000).

Two enemies, played by Branko Djuric (left) and Rene Bitorajac (right), look to their own lines for safety in *No Man's Land* (2001).

Movie 39: *No Man's Land*

Director: Danis Tanovic; 1 hour, 37 minutes; 2001—Winner of the Oscar for Best Foreign Film
Watch the movie.

Questions to Ponder:

1. *No Man's Land* shows both the deep divisions between combatants from opposite sides of a war, and the tendency for those divisions to break down when enemies meet face-to-face and start to communicate. Nino (Rene Bitorajac) and Ciki (Branko Djuric) start to communicate when they discuss the girl Ciki dated, the girl who attended Nino's school. What factors interrupted that communication and led them again to become mortal foes?

2. The film shows the questionable behavior of some UNPROFOR

decision-makers and of members of the media covering the war. What should UNPROFOR do about the situation involving Cera (Filip Sovogovic)? Are they wrong to pretend they are transporting a wounded Cera to a hospital? If the reporter, Jane Livingston (Katrin Cartlidge), had discovered that Cera was still lying on the bomb, what would she have done? How would she have reported this tragedy? A friend of mine thinks Livingston *knew* Cera had not been saved, do you agree with my friend?

ADDITIONAL RECOMMENDATIONS FOR WAR

The Bridge on the River Kwai (1957). Watching this movie makes you want to whistle its famous melody. Academy awards for Best Picture, Best Director (David Lean), Best Actor (Alec Guinness), Best Score, Best Adapted Screenplay, Best Cinematography, and Best Editing. It deserved all these, and it stands the test of time as one of the best war movies. David Lean also directed *Lawrence of Arabia* and *Dr. Zhivago*, two other great epics.

Apocalypse Now Redux (2001). With 55 additional minutes, is *Redux* better than the original theatrical release? If you are so inclined, watch both and decide for yourself. An excellent documentary on the making of the film is *Hearts of Darkness — A Filmmaker's Apocalypse* (1991). The plot of *Apocalypse Now* is loosely based on Joseph Conrad's *Heart of Darkness*. Given the difficulties encountered during filming, it is almost a miracle it was completed. The scenes of Robert Duvall on the beach and the sounds of Richard Wagner's "Ride of the Valkyries" as a backdrop to a helicopter raid against the Viet Cong are unforgettable.

The Deer Hunter (1978). Literally a movie in three acts. Act I captures the togetherness of a Pennsylvania community just before two of its citizens, close friends Michael (Robert DeNiro) and Nick (Christopher Walken), leave for Vietnam. Act II centers on the experiences of Michael and Nick in Vietnam. In Act III the viewer witnesses the results of the physical and psychological wounds of the war.

Platoon (1986). A quick glimpse of body bags at the beginning of *Platoon* is a sobering sight. The film is known for its accuracy in portraying the confusion of bush fighting in Vietnam. I feel the plot makes an unrealistic turn near the end when the good sergeant, Elias (Willem Dafoe), and the bad staff sergeant (Tom Berenger) meet in mortal combat.

They Came to Cordura (1959). Centers on the nature of bravery and cowardice. It would be interesting to watch this in conjunction with *The Red Badge of Courage* (Movie 35).

All Quiet on the Western Front (1930): Suggestion: Read Erich Maria Remarque's novel first. The 1930 film version is much better than a 1979 remake. Lew Ayres stars in the original version and appears also in the remake. Winner of the Best Picture and Best Director Oscars for 1930. The last scene of the film is haunting.

The Horse Soldiers (1959). One of the John Ford/John Wayne films. Based on the Grierson Raid into Mississippi in 1863 during the Civil War. The film suffers when Wayne's character falls for a Southern belle (played by Constance Towers) who looks like she came right off the set of the *Ozzie and Harriet* show.

Glory (1989). Matthew Broderick, in one of his better roles, shines as Robert Gould Shaw, the colonel of the Regiment of the Massachusetts Volunteer Infantry. The glory is that won by blacks fighting for their own freedom during the Civil War. The film captures the unbelievable courage of their attack on South Carolina's Fort Wagner, but shies away from the atrocities that befell any who became Confederate prisoners. Denzel Washington won a Best Supporting Actor Oscar. The quality of his performance is matched by that of Morgan Freeman.

Johnny Got His Gun (1971). Fans of the heavy metal group Metallica have undoubtedly seen clips of this movie in the band's music video for the song "One." I recommend reading Dalton Trumbo's novel of the same name before viewing the film.

Good Morning, Vietnam (1987). Robin Williams won the Best Actor Oscar for his role as a controversial radio disc jockey serving troops in Vietnam. Director Barry Levinson permitted Williams to improvise quite a bit.

Grand Illusion (1938). There are many good prisoner of war movies, including *The Bridge on the River Kwai* (see earlier entry), *Stalag 17* (1953), and *The Great Escape* (1963). *Grand Illusion* may be the grandest of them all.

11

Racism

In some of my sections from "Introduction to Philosophy," I tell students I assign final grades in what they may think is a strange way. I ask all students wearing blue to raise their hands. I then announce that since blue is an "average" color, all those who raised their hands will receive a "C" in the course. Students wearing red will merit an "A" grade. Students wearing other colors will be assigned other grades. Since many of my students have been programmed to be ethical relativists who claim "no one can *know* what is good and what is bad," I use this color example to get them to admit they know giving a course grade based on the color of clothes worn is not good. (Of course, the "A"s will waver somewhat.) Not only does my example tend to undermine ethical relativism, it also provides an avenue to attack judgments of merit based on racist beliefs. If clothing color should not be considered in passing judgment on people, why should the color of skin? Any person — including the racist — will immediately know a wrong is being committed when he or she is judged on the basis of something as irrelevant as skin color. An excellent example is provided in *The Long Walk Home* (Movie 44) when Whoopi Goldberg's character is called "nigger," or when she is forced to ride in the back of the bus. The expression on Goldberg's face as she is treated with such disrespect tells so much. People *need* to feel respected. If people are not respected because of their ethnic background, they may not be granted equal rights before the law, they may be discriminated against when applying for jobs, and their education will too often be inferior to that of the ruling class. (Just think of slaves in America who were not permitted to learn to read; an educated person who is denied rights can become a dangerous person to his or her tormentors.)

Shoah (Movie 46) provides excellent evidence to support the idea that racists know they are on flimsy moral footing. Claude Lanzmann interviews villagers who lived next to a concentration camp — villagers who deny any responsibility for the Holocaust. Watch their faces. Listen as some who start to express guilt are silenced by others.

Movie 40: *The Birth of a Nation*

Director: D. W. Griffith; 3 hours, 7 minutes; 1915

All the other movies in this chapter are, to a great extent, critical of racism. *The Birth of a Nation*, on the other hand, is based on a racist play entitled *The Clansman* by Thomas Dixon, Jr., and is a masterpiece of filmmaking by the great director D. W. Griffith, himself a racist. Probably no other film has so blatantly projected images that depict African-Americans as, at best, buffoons and, at worst, sexual predators. The Ku Klux Klan is portrayed as the group that will save America. It is no wonder that the NAACP has regularly protested against the film.

The Birth of a Nation, despite disgusting content, deserves to be preserved, viewed, and discussed. Why? Because it almost single-handedly set the movie business on the road to what it is today. The film is epic

A disturbing scene from D.W. Griffith's *The Birth of a Nation* (1915).

in proportion and has been viewed by uncounted millions of people. Except for the unforgivable racist stereotypes and the warped romanticizing of the Ku Klux Klan, *The Birth of a Nation* contains stunning scenes of recreated battles and other historic events, including the assassination of Abraham Lincoln. There is the drama of young men, North and South, marching off to do battle with one another. There are the women left behind. The devastation of the South and its citizens' fear for the future is vividly presented. With the film, D.W. Griffith brought to the screen numerous innovations. The movie is a classic and deserves to be listed on the National Film Registry, as it was in 1992. The NAACP protested against the Library of Congress for placing it in that Registry. However, the film was granted such an honor not because the Library of Congress promotes racist views, but because of its central place in film history.

Watch the movie.

Questions to ponder:

1. Do you think a person who considers *The Birth of a Nation* a great movie must be either racist or stupid? If that is your opinion, have you searched for the *merits* of the film? Because there are many! What scenes disgusted you most? Why?

2. Though I am convinced most racists *know* their belief and behavior is immoral, they can't admit it because they don't want to give up the power they possess over the oppressed and they don't want to face ostracism from friends and family if they begin to change their views. In addition, when racist beliefs are institutionalized, they begin to seem natural. So when *The Birth of a Nation* first appeared, most viewers probably did not center their attention on the immoral depiction of African-Americans. They would have been stunned by the cinematic experience.[1] Do you currently accept the stereotyping of certain groups of people — stereotyping that will be obvious in future generations?

Movie 41: *Mississippi Burning*

Director: Alan Parker; 2 hours, 7 minutes; 1988

In June 1964, James Chaney, Andrew Goodman and Mickey Schwerner, three young Civil Rights workers, arrived in Mississippi. They were there to join hundreds of others trying to help local black people

Gene Hackman (left) and Willem Dafoe (right) seek the murderers of three Civil Rights workers in *Mississippi Burning* (1988).

organize in the fight to end segregation. Shortly after arriving, the three disappeared. Six weeks later their bodies were recovered from an earthen dam. The broader story of "Freedom Summer," as well as an in-depth account of the murders of the three civil rights workers and the subsequent investigation, is covered in the excellent book *We Are Not Afraid: The Story of Goodman, Schwerner, and Chaney and the Civil Rights Campaign for Mississippi* by Seth Cagin and Philip Dray (New York: Macmillan, 1988). I recommend reading the book before watching the highly fictionalized *Mississippi Burning*.

     Watch the movie.

Questions to ponder:

     1. Alan Parker, the director of the film, admits the plot contains fictional elements in the account of the murders of Chaney, Goodman and Schwerner, and the aftermath of those murders. The factual sections of the film are extremely well done. Indeed, several scenes, including the opening one, are unforgettable. (The image of cars traveling in the dark

over rolling hills has stuck with me since I first viewed the film in 1988.) Though the fictional story is always interesting — especially when Gene Hackman's character is onscreen — Parker perpetrates an injustice by almost totally ignoring the role of blacks in the events he portrays. One comes away from the film thinking that only white FBI agents played a role in the events of 1964. One critic put it this way: "The blacks in *Mississippi Burning* tremble in fear of whites, disband their conversations whenever whites approach and retreat in mute submission. There is one brave black child who stands up, but no one else.... In *Mississippi Burning*, black people ... sing movement spirituals like 'Precious Lord' (at the beginning) and 'Walk On' (at the end), but otherwise they don't count."[2] Do you agree that the movie minimizes the role of blacks as outlined above? Did you spot this discrepancy as you watched the movie, or did you need it pointed out to you?

2. Ward (Willem Dafoe) asks: "Where does it come from — all this hatred?" Anderson (Gene Hackman) then tells the story of Monroe's mule. Anderson's father killed the mule because mules were "big deals at that time." Does the Monroe story answer Ward's question concerning the source of racial hatred? Do racists *know* they are wrong? After all, Anderson's father was ashamed when he realized his son knew he had killed the mule.

3. The Confederate flag pops up numerous times in the film. Should *Mississippi Burning* give pause to those who think the Confederate flag is not necessarily a symbol of a racist point of view?

Movie 42: *American History X*

Director: Tony Kaye; 1 hour, 59 minutes; 1998

Warning: This film contains some very disturbing scenes of violence.

Watch the movie.

Questions to ponder:

1. Is it true that human beings have to learn to be racist? Can they "unlearn" their beliefs? Bob Sweeney (Avery Brooks), the black school teacher, thinks such unlearning is possible.

2. Sweeney asks Derek (Edward Norton) if anything he has done has made his life better. Is that a good question to ask a racist? Why or

Edward Norton stars in *American History X* (1998).

why not? How would you respond if a racist answers: "Yes — hating these people?"

3. Would Derek have undergone his radical character change if Sweeney hadn't been there to influence him or if he had not been thrown together with the black prisoner in the laundry room (Guy Torry)? Would Danny (Edward Furlong) have written his report for Sweeney if Derek had not undergone such a radical change? Do Derek and Danny's character changes support the deterministic viewpoint?

Movie 43: *Do the Right Thing*

Director: Spike Lee; 2 hours; 1989
Watch the movie.

Questions to ponder:

1. Vincent Canby, film critic for the *New York Times*, said Sal (Danny Aiello) "is the film's richest, most complex character."[3] Do you agree with that assessment? Why or why not?

Mookie (Spike Lee, left) and Sal (Danny Aiello, right) have a friendly (?) chat in *Do the Right Thing* (1989).

2. Sal says to Mookie (Spike Lee): "You've always been like a son to me." Was Sal serious? Was Sal like a father to Mookie?

3. Should Sal have put some pictures of famous African-Americans on the wall of his pizzeria? Was Buggin Out (Giancarlo Esposito) justified in attempting to organize a boycott because there were only photos of Italian-Americans on the wall?

4. Is *Do the Right Thing* a "sanitized portrait of ghetto life," as one critic suggested?[4]

5. When *Do the Right Thing* was first released, it generated a major controversy. Nice guy Mookie starts the riot when he throws the garbage can through the window of the pizzeria. People seemed more disturbed by Mookie's action than by the killing of Radio Raheem (Bill Nunn). Does that make sense? Does Mookie "do the right thing?" Do any other characters do the right thing?

6. Roger Ebert writes: "Thoughtless people have accused Lee over the years of being an angry filmmaker. He has much to be angry about,

but I don't find it in his work. The wonder of *Do the Right Thing* is that he is so fair."[5] Do you agree with Ebert's judgment?

Further recommendation:

If you enjoyed *Do the Right Thing*, see Spike Lee's *Malcolm X*. Denzel Washington shines in the starring role.

Movie 44: *The Long Walk Home*

Director: Richard Pearce; 1 hour, 38 minutes; 1990
Watch the movie.

Questions to ponder:

1. Norma Thompson (Sissy Spacek) slowly becomes aware of the injustice of segregation. What factors lead her to this awareness? Why doesn't her husband (Dwight Schultz) or her brother-in-law (Dylan Baker) follow the same path?

2. Odessa (Whoopi Goldberg) tells Norma that if she joins the car-

Odessa (Whoopi Goldberg) on *The Long Walk Home* (1991).

pool, she may never be able to "step back." That is, once Norma joins the Civil Rights Movement, she will never again desire to support segregation, and many of her close (racist) acquaintances will turn their backs on her. Why would few people who become enlightened about the evils of racism ever "step back" to it?

3. Norma admits she is scared. Odessa tells her, "We're all scared. But what's scaring you, Miss Thompson — who you are or who Mr. Thompson wants you to be?" List the things that might frighten someone like Norma who is evolving from being a racist toward being someone who accepts all people as equals?

4. There is one word in the quote from question 3 that stands out for me in a very special way. Odessa calls Norma "*Miss* Thompson." Norma calls Odessa by her first name. Norma can be familiar with Odessa, but not vice versa. I have been called "sir" by a number of African-Americans, but I seldom hear African-American adult males called "sir" by white adults. "Sir" is a sign of respect. If an African-American says to me, "Pardon me, sir," I feel I am being shown respect. If an African-American male only hears a white adult say "Pardon me," he must know respect is not being shown. Can you think of any other types of behavior that may indicate that traces of racism are still hanging around, even in supposedly enlightened human beings?

Movie 45: *Imitation of Life*

Director: Douglas Sirk; 2 hours, 5 minutes; 1959

If you have never seen a film directed by Douglas Sirk, you may not be ready for one — yet. His movies are *ultra*-melodramatic. I recommend first watching the wonderful Todd Haynes film, *Far from Heaven*, an art theater success and critical hit from 2002, starring Julianne Moore and Dennis Quaid. Haynes captures Sirk's style. In fact, *Far from Heaven* is a remake of Sirk's 1956 film, *All That Heaven Allows*. Watch that latter film after viewing *Far from Heaven*. In *All That Heaven Allows*, not only will you be reintroduced to two superstars of yesteryear, Jane Wyman and Rock Hudson, but you will now start to enter Sirk's world. *Then* turn to *Imitation of Life*.

The 1959 film is itself a remake of 1934's *Imitation of Life*. The earlier version is more faithful to the Fannie Hurst novel on which it is based. Watching *that* movie after watching Sirk's version is also fun.

Lana Turner (left) and Juanita Moore (right) star in *Imitation of Life* (1959).

In the Sirk version, the two main characters are Laura Meredith (Lana Turner) and Annie Johnson (Juanita Moore). Laura is white and Annie is African-American. At the beginning of the film we are introduced to Laura, Annie and their young daughters, who are supposed to be sweet things but seem like brats to me. After viewing several important plot developments, we are transported ten years into the future. Lana Turner still portrays Laura and Juanita Moore is still Annie. Sandra Dee is now the teenage Susie and Susan Kohner is Sarah. Sandra Dee brings to mind a kewpie doll. Sarah's father was white, and she appears to be white. The fact that she is Annie's daughter causes her a great deal of grief. (In the 1934 version, Annie's daughter was played more authentically by bi-racial actress Fredi Washington.)

Highlights in the film: Juanita Moore's moving performance, and the bad acting by just about everyone else except, perhaps, John Gavin. Near the end of the movie there is a wonderful performance by Mahalia Jackson singing "Trouble of the World."

Watch the movie.

Questions to ponder:

1. The title song is sung nicely by Earl Grant. What significance do the opening lyrics have in the film? What characters, if any, are living an "Imitation of Life"?

2. Laura tells the rebelling Sarah Jane: "Have I ever treated you differently [than I treated my own daughter]?" Had she? Was Laura's relationship with Annie a relationship of equals?

3. For a movie made in 1959, before the Civil Rights Movement, *Imitation of Life* was ahead of its time. A single mother raising children, and a bi-racial girl dating an (unsuspecting) white boy, are not topics Hollywood readily addressed at that time. However, there still seems to be some stereotyping in the film. If you agree, point out some of the stereotyping.

ADDITIONAL RECOMMENDATIONS FOR EXPLORING RACISM IN FILM

4 Little Girls (1998). On September 15, 1963, in Birmingham, Alabama, a bomb goes off next to a black Baptist Church, killing four little girls. Spike Lee's documentary takes us back to that painful time.

Guess Who's Coming to Dinner? (1967). Katharine Hepburn, Sidney Poitier, and Spencer Tracy star in Stanley Kramer's movie about upper class white parents coming to grips with the fact that their daughter is planning to marry a black doctor. Hepburn won the Oscar for Best Actress for her role as the mother.

Mississippi Masala (1992). Guess which African-American actor wants to come to an Indian dinner? Stars Sarita Choudhury, Roshan Seth (who played Nehru in *Gandhi*), and Denzel Washington.

12

The Holocaust

The question arises as to whether film can truly capture the horror of the Holocaust. How is it possible to portray the systematic murder of seven million people? The amount of suffering and grief seems incomprehensible. However, the first two films in this chapter (*Shoah* and *The Pianist*) are great works that are successful on numerous counts. *Shoah*, a documentary over nine hours in length, centers on unforgettable testimony given by survivors, but contains no wartime footage. *The Pianist* won Academy Awards for Best Director (Roman Polanski), Best Actor (Adrien Brody) and Best Screenplay. Polanski, himself a Holocaust survivor, shows the step-by-step dehumanization of the Jewish population of Warsaw, as well as what life was like in the Warsaw Ghetto. Too many Holocaust films seem to be escape-against-all-odds adventure/action movies. Based on memoirs by Wladyslaw Szpilman, *The Pianist* is nothing at all like these action movies.

The third film in this chapter (*Mr. Death*) is a documentary about a "Holocaust denier." The fourth picture is Roberto Benigni's *Life Is Beautiful*.

A book I highly recommend is Martin Gilbert's *The Holocaust: A History of the Jews of Europe During the Second World War* (New York: Holt Rinehart and Winston, 1986). It is an excellent survey of the entire period of the Holocaust and is a work that supplements the movies you watch. Gilbert expertly weaves the testimony of survivors into a chronological history of the Holocaust.

Movie 46: *Shoah*

Director: Claude Lanzmann; 9 hours, 46 minutes; 1985

Shoah is one of the great documentaries in the history of cinema. Claude Lanzmann is the genius behind the film. He has included testi-

From *Shoah* (1985): Simon Srebnik, survivor of Chelmno, meeting with Polish residents of Chelmno forty years later.

mony of survivors, as well as that of some of the perpetrators. As one atrocity after another is recounted, viewers will find many moments that are painful to listen to and painful to watch. It is utterly distressful to hear bureaucrats claiming they didn't know what was going on, particularly when their behavior and the expressions on their faces show that they are lying.

Shoah is a long movie. I think certain segments could have been shortened. Too many trains are shown. Some witnesses speak in their native language, but we don't find out what they are saying until a translator interprets for Lanzmann (and then we are presented with subtitles). It would have been better to have included the subtitles *as they spoke*. Also, the last hour loses some steam.

No wartime footage is included in *Shoah*. However, you will feel that you are there in 1940s Treblinka, Auschwitz and Sobibor. Many survivors are reluctant to articulate their memories because those memories put them back into the horror. Their words and the depth of their sadness convey to the viewer some sense of the horror they experienced.

Watch the movie.

Questions to ponder:

1. Does *Shoah* successfully debunk the claim of various civilians and bureaucrats that they "didn't know about the attempted extermination of the Jews?" What interviews were most forceful in this respect?

2. Raul Hilberg, a great historian of the Holocaust, claims in his interview that the "Final Solution" was the "logical progression" from what came before. As he put it, from "the fourth century … the missionaries of Christianity had said in effect to the Jews: 'You may not live among us as Jews.' The secular rulers who followed them from the late Middle Ages then decided: 'You may not live among us'; and the Nazis finally decreed: 'You may not live.'" From what you know, do you agree with Hilberg that the Holocaust was a logical progression from what came before?

3. For me, one of the most haunting scenes is the one in which Simon Srebnik, the survivor who at thirteen sang for the Germans and sang on the river, is surrounded by the villagers of Chelmno. What could Srebnik be thinking? The villagers act like his friends. But when he was there as a child, no Pole stood up to help him. How can they stand next to him and smile as if a long lost friend had shown up?

4. Another very difficult scene to watch contains the testimony of the barber, Abraham Bomba. He tells of another barber who had to cut the hair of his wife and daughter just prior to their entering the gas chamber. Why do questions utilitarians would ordinarily ask seem absurd in this situation? (For example, consider this question: Should the wife and daughter be told that death awaits them? Would "a greater amount of happiness arise" if they were told the truth?)

5. How much responsibility for the Holocaust should the following persons accept?

    a. Engineers of the trains that carried victims to the concentration camps.

    b. The head of Mittel Europaisch Reiseburo, the official travel bureau, which — for a profit — according to Hilberg, would "ship people to the gas chambers or … ship vacationers to their favorite resort."

    c. Dr. Franz Grassler, deputy to Dr. Auerswald, Nazi Commissioner of the Warsaw Ghetto, who regularly tells Lanzmann such things as, "You're asking more than I know. The policy that wound up with extermination, the 'Final Solution'—we knew nothing about it, of course."

An additional recommendation: After finishing *Shoah*, it would be good to watch *The Last Days* (1998). *The Last Days* interviews survivors, but also offers wartime footage.

Movie 47: *The Pianist*

Director: Roman Polanski; 2 hours, 28 minutes; 2002

The Pianist is not an ordinary Holocaust movie. When director Roman Polanski was seven years old, he escaped from the Krakow ghetto. He knows firsthand the terrors and atrocities committed by the Nazi regime. From that knowledge, sets were carefully prepared for the movie—sets that capture Warsaw in the 1930s and 1940s. Polanski traces the details of the systematic dehumanization of Warsaw's Jewish population. There was something uplifting about *Schindler's List*; a good person saves many Jews. There is little uplifting about *The Pianist*; the movie

Adrien Brody as Wladyslaw Szpilman, *The Pianist* (2002).

shows what little hope there was for the Jews of Warsaw during World War II.

Watch the movie.

Questions to ponder:

1. What decisions did the members of the family of Wladyslaw Szpilman (Adrien Brody) make in the first part of the movie that fated them to suffer and perish at the hands of the Nazis? Should they have known what was in store for them? If not, why?

2. Is the following a flaw in the movie? There are good Poles and bad Poles, but the viewer never knows what happens to them subsequent to their actions that either help or harm Jews. What happened to Jews who collaborated with the Nazis? The viewer does learn that the German captain (Thomas Kretschmann), who appears near the end of the film, does not survive. Some critics think the scenes with the captain are overly sentimental. What do you think?

Movie 48: *Mr. Death*

Director: Errol Morris; 1 hour, 32 minutes; 1999
Watch the movie.

Questions to ponder:

1. Should it be illegal to deny in print that the Holocaust ever occurred? Why or why not?

2. Is someone who denies the Holocaust necessarily an anti–Semite? (If someone denies blacks were ever enslaved in the United States, would that person necessarily have racist views about blacks?) Is Leuchter shown to be an anti–Semite by his desecration of the "holy ground" of Auschwitz? Was he clearly an anti–Semite because he spoke to organizations that were anti-Semitic? Does the word "evil" fit Leuchter?

3. Given the testimonies in *Shoah*, the great number of photographs and testimony of other survivors, the records in archives (such as those found at Auschwitz), etc., how can *anyone* deny the Holocaust occurred and still be considered a rational being?

Fred A. Leuchter, Jr., is *Mr. Death* (1999).

Movie 49: *Life Is Beautiful*

Director: Roberto Benigni; 1 hour, 56 minutes; 1998
Watch the movie.

A question to ponder:

1. Viewers of *Life Is Beautiful* should attempt to answer the following major question: Is Roberto Benigni's movie an immoral coupling of slapstick humor with the unspeakable horror of the Holocaust? Nowhere in *Shoah* will you find survivors mentioning humorous events occurring in the camps. Also, some claim that Guido's saving of his son's life may lead to the irrational conclusion that one could have reasonably felt hope while in a concentration camp, and that a child could be kept from realizing the horrors of his surroundings. There was no hope, and children could not be kept from the horror.

Comments:

My view is that Benigni succeeds in capturing some of the horror of the Holocaust. When Guido stumbles upon the huge stack of human

Giorgio Cantarini (left) and Roberto Benigni (right) in *Life Is Beautiful* (1998).

corpses, reality sets in. When early in the movie an anti–Semitic sign suddenly appears ("No Jews or Dogs Allowed"), the peace that Guido and his family deserve is shattered, and the viewers who have enjoyed following Guido's story are shocked.

The power of one particular scene did not move me as much during my first viewing as during my second and third. The scene is the now-famous sequence in which Guido jauntily marches past the box in which his son hides. Knowing this good man is marching to his death — and he knows it also — brings home the unspeakable brutality of the Nazis.

Another scene that stands out is the one in which Guido makes fun of the absurd idea of the "pure Italian." That scene matches the quality of Charlie Chaplin lambasting Adolf Hitler in *The Great Dictator*.

ADDITIONAL RECOMMENDATIONS
FOR FILMS ON THE HOLOCAUST

Hotel Terminus: The Life and Times of Klaus Barbie (1988). Barbie was the head of the Gestapo in Lyon, France. This four-hour-plus documentary by Marcel Ophuls captures the rise and fall of "the Butcher of Lyon." Barbie was one of the most sought-after Nazi war criminals. For forty years he escaped justice. The story of his capture is a critical part of *Hotel Terminus.*

Night and Fog (1956). This early documentary is only 32 minutes in length. The "Night" of the Holocaust years was followed by the "Fog" of the early post-war years when the responsibility for — and the immensity of— the suffering experienced during the Holocaust was not adequately addressed.

Schindler's List (1993). With this film, Steven Spielberg showed his savvy by making an important movie outside the realm of fantasy cinema. (His earlier *The Color Purple* [Movie 25] contained too much slapstick for a serious movie.) Liam Neeson won the Best Actor Oscar for his role as Schindler, and Spielberg won as Best Director.

Into the Arms of Strangers: Stories of the Kindertransport (2000). The Academy Award–winning documentary on the 10,000-plus children sent to safety in Great Britain by their Jewish parents trapped in Hitler's grip.

Sophie's Choice (1982). Sophie (Meryl Streep) is faced with a choice placed on her by a demonic Nazi concentration camp guard. The story focuses on the aftereffects of her choice, years after she is rescued from the concentration camp.

The Grey Zone (2001). *The Grey Zone* is perhaps the most difficult to watch of all the fictional films about the Holocaust. The actors speak in a monotone, à la *House of Games* (Movie 3). Little attempt is made to select actors from nationalities included in the plot. However, without exception, the acting is superb. Harvey Keitel plays the commandant of Auschwitz. David Arquette and Steve Buscemi shine as members of the Sondercommand. Mia Sorvino also gives an outstanding performance. You will never forget the portion of the film that deals with an attempt to save one young girl in the midst of unspeakable death.

Gloomy Sunday (1999). A ménage à quatre (that's one more than a ménage à trois) in the midst of the Holocaust.

13

Sexism and Women's Issues

Human beings need to possess a healthy self-esteem and to feel self-actualized. In a male-dominated culture, it is the male who has these feelings and it is the male who makes sure the female does not have them. Women's rights issues are regularly attracting attention, and, at least in "enlightened" cultures, women are making major inroads into domains controlled by men since time immemorial.

A thorough presentation of contemporary women's issues is beyond the boundaries of this book. Books by Joan Jacobs Brumberg, Susan Faludi, Betty Freidan, Camille Paglia, Gloria Steinem, and Naomi Wolf can help fill in the details.

This chapter contains one film that focuses on the issue of abortion (*If These Walls Could Talk — Part I*). Most of the other movies deal with women and the difficulties they face in a world in which men have most of the power. Throughout the ages, women were led to believe they were unfit for any number of fulfilling occupations. The standard judgment was that women could not be philosophers because they were mainly guided by emotion, and the rational part of their souls remained underdeveloped. They couldn't be artists (see Movie 55 —*Artemisia*). Only men could be warriors or leaders (see Movie 56 — *Whale Rider*). Of course, they could be mothers and nurses and serve the needs of men. Women were often thought of as mere sex objects — to be used and then discarded. The abuse women have suffered at the hands of males is not just physical abuse. Many women have been pushed down until their psyches are deeply wounded (see Movie 50—*In the Company of Men* and Movie 52 —*Ladybird, Ladybird*).

I believe the best explanation for many of the wrongs done to women — wrongs addressed in several of the movies included here — to be found in the great classic analysis of the nature of women, *The Second Sex* by Simone de Beauvoir. Perhaps de Beauvoir does not provide enough guidance on how women can achieve empowerment, but I still feel she well describes many of the root causes of the oppression of women — causes that are still at work in the world today.

In *The Second Sex*, one finds chapters that analyze different stages of a female's life. These include "Childhood," "The Young Girl," "Sexual Initiation," "The Married Woman," "The Mother," and "From Maturity to Old Age." Some of the elements of those stages, according to de Beauvoir, are as follows:

1. Childhood: The female child will immediately be treated differently than the male child, and that difference will have a lifelong effect on the female. The girl will not be granted the level of independence granted to the boy. The boy will be treated as if "great things are in store for him."[1] Girls are expected to be the more passive sex; boys the more active.

> "Climbing trees, fighting with his companions, facing them in rough games, he feels his body as a means for dominating nature and as a weapon for fighting; he takes pride in his muscles as in his sex; in games, sports, fights, challenges, feats of strength, he finds a balanced exercise of his powers; at the same time he absorbs the severe lessons of violence; he learns from an early age to take blows, to scorn pain, to keep back the tears."[2]

The female child, on the other hand, is taught that her place in life is to exist for others. She "plays house," has baby dolls, and dresses up "to look pretty." Playing with dolls prepares her for when she will have a living doll of her own. Playing house prepares her for being the organizer of a real house.

By the time the child approaches puberty, her body undergoes changes that excite and frighten her.

> "Arms, legs, skin, muscles, even the rounded bottom on which she sits — up to now, all these have had their obvious usefulness; only her sex, clearly a urinary organ, has seemed to be somewhat dubious, but secret and invisible to others. Under her sweater or blouse, her breasts make their display, and the body becomes an object that others see and pay attention to."[3]

She can be excited by the change, but she also begins to feel that she is viewed as an object. Shame becomes part of the experience of her body.

Menstruation begins. A young girl is made aware of the age-old judgment that a female's menstruation is "unclean."

2. The Young Girl: Boys continue to play rough games. There is wrestling and football. The girl continues to feel weaker and weaker — and vulnerable. "The young girl is expected to repress her spontaneity and replace it with the studied grace and charm taught her by her elders."[4] The young man is expected to be independent. Boys do things; girls daydream. Girls are frightened of boys, but attach themselves to some "safe" male — a movie star or pop singer. His picture is taped on the wall next to her bed. She would care for "him"; he would be wonderful to her. He is her "distant Prince Charming."

Makeup is now applied. The young girl "is now only an offered flower, a fruit to be picked."[5]

3. Sexual Initiation: Men look at young women whose development shows they are physically ready for sexual initiation. That look frightens women. (Both de Beauvoir and Jean-Paul Sartre write about "the look." The way another person looks at us tells us we are being viewed *as a thing*. The developed female is looked at, and the female knows she is seen as a sexual object.) The woman who has been programmed to be non-aggressive is now penetrated by a man who has been programmed to be aggressive. All too often, the sexual act, even if consensual, appears to the female to be a violation.

4. The Married Woman: Persons usually enter into a marriage thinking they are in love. However, even if they are in love, "it rarely persists through the long years to come."[6] The female finds that her possibilities in a male-dominated world are extremely limited. The home becomes a prison.

5. The Mother: It is difficult to generalize about the effect of motherhood on women. The man needs her to do this and that. Now a child needs her. Many women experience joy at "being needed." Others, however, are frustrated by their lot as a woman in a world where women do not count for much. "She will seek to compensate for all these frustrations through her child." Knowing about those frustrations, an independent observer could be "frightened at the thought that defenseless infants are abandoned to her care." [7] A mother merely "makes herself the slave of her offspring to compensate for the emptiness of her heart..."[8] As the child grows and becomes more and more independent, the mother may start to feel her purpose in life is being lost.

6. From Maturity to Old Age: The aging woman feels the toll the years exact from her body. In a society that stresses youth and youthful

beauty, the woman feels left behind. She sees her options limited, compared to those possessed by the male. There is a chance, now that she has fulfilled her duties as wife and mother, that she can experience freedom. However, she finds this freedom "at the very time when she can make no use of it."[9] She ends up "killing time." (De Beauvoir does admit there are exceptions to this generalization, but they are extremely rare.)

In the movies covered in this chapter, you will meet characters who are kept down because they are women. You will often be able to spot causes of abuse that have been mentioned in de Beauvoir's account presented above. At times, you will witness the tragic step-by-step destruction of the female psyche. In several of the films, however, women achieve a state of self-actualization.

Movie 50: *In the Company of Men*

Director: Neil Labute; 1 hour, 37 minutes; 1997
Warning: Extreme nastiness.
Watch the movie.

Aaron Eckhart (left) and Matt Malloy (right) in a scene from *The Company of Men* (1997).

Questions to ponder:

1. Chad (Aaron Eckhart) wants to "restore a little dignity" to his life, not only by hurting Christine (Stacy Edwards), but, as it turns out, by hurting Howard (Matt Malloy) as well. The young black worker whom Chad humiliates is another example of one of his victims. What leads Chad to be so hurtful? Does his type of occupation, which stresses power, have anything to do with it? Would a company of women be any different?

2. Howard clearly feels remorse for his part in the plot to hurt Christine. He has even fallen for Christine. Should she have forgiven him?

3. Suppose you are hired to write a sequel to *In the Company of Men*. In the sequel, events occur that lead Chad to realize there is a higher dignity than any attained by hurting people. How would your plot proceed?

Movie 51: *Thelma and Louise*

Director: Ridley Scott; 2 hours, 9 minutes; 1991
Warning: Contains one particularly disturbing scene!
Watch the movie.

Questions to ponder:

1. Louise (Susan Sarandon) had been raped in the past. She knew that without physical evidence the claim that she and Thelma (Geena Davis) had acted in self-defense in Harlan's murder would not be believed. Given the fact that the killing took place after the sexual assault had been disrupted, and Harlan shouted obscenities at Louise, does the claim of self-defense ring true? If Louise had not shot Harlan, what should she and Thelma have done following the sexual assault? What should they have done following the murder?

2. Here is part of the conversation between the sexist trucker and Thelma and Louise — a conversation that occurs prior to the destruction of his truck:

> THELMA: "We think you have really bad manners."
> TRUCKER (laughing proudly): "Yeh!"
> LOUISE: "How would you feel if someone did that to your mother? Or your sister? Your wife?"
> TRUCKER (puzzled): "Huh? What are you talkin' about?"

Susan Sarandon (left) and Geena Davis (right) take aim in *Thelma and Louise* (1991).

LOUISE: "You know good and damn well what I'm talking about."
TRUCKER: "You women are crazy."

The trucker does not seem to have a clue that his behavior is repulsive. Indeed, he thinks Thelma and Louise must be "crazy" to say the things they are saying. But Louise claims he knows what they are taking about. Is Louise right? Does he know? Suppose instead of this sexist trucker there were another sexist male who was more intelligent. That male would probably also fail to be moved by the question Louise asks. Why would such a rational question probably fail to motivate *any* sexist male to correct his ways?

3. Did you notice a number of "existential themes" (Chapter 4 — Anxiety and Inauthenticity) in *Thelma and Louise*? These two ordinary women — kept down by the sexist society they live in — reach a state of existential freedom. Louise says, "Something crossed over in me; I just can't go back." At another time, Thelma says she has "never felt so awake." If they could have turned back time, they would not have been involved in a murder. But even given their situation, they achieve a state of authenticity and will a fuller life than they had ever experienced before. They

even choose what Nietzsche would call a "free death."[10] Their death is too life-confirming to be called a suicide. Would *you* call what was shown in the last scene an "act of suicide?"

Movie 52: *Ladybird, Ladybird*

Director: Ken Loach; 1 hour, 42 minutes; 1995
Warning: Contains explicit scenes of women being abused and other heart-wrenching elements, and some disturbing language. It will be as difficult for most American viewers to understand the thick British accents as it would be for most British viewers to understand Snoop Doggy Dog or Lyndon Johnson.
Watch the movie.

Questions to ponder:

1. In *About Schmidt* (Movie 11), Schmidt's daughter is marrying a real bumpkin. Why can't she see through him? Time after time, Maggie (Crissy Rock) falls into relationships with abusive men. Why? Part of the explanation, it seems to me, is provided in a work on the nature of romantic love written by the great novelist Stendhal. He claims that when we romantically fall in love we project "crystals" onto the loved one. Crystals are beautiful perfections. The loved one does not really possess these perfections, but the lover projecting them cannot see that the loved one is really, at best, an ordinary person, and at worst, a violent, controlling demon.[11] This "crystallization theory," however, can only provide part of the explanation. What other factors lead some women into abusive relationships?

At the beginning of the previous paragraph, I asked why neither Schmidt's daughter nor Maggie can spot that the match they are about to enter into is not one in their self-interest. A common answer is that "appearances can be deceiving." The lover is *acting* while the relationship is forming, but the real person will surface when the other party becomes trapped in the relationship. I have difficulty with this explanation. People will say you can't tell what a person is like from their appearance, but I think you can. I agree with the great philosopher Schopenhauer, who holds that the appearance is not separate from reality. It is obvious from the appearance of Jorge (Vladimir Vega), that he is a good

Crissy Rock stars in *Ladybird, Ladybird* (1995).

man! His smile shows it! Randall's behavior in *About Schmidt* shows he is someone who will not help his lover grow. Beware of a person who throws empty beer cans out the window of a pickup truck — a pickup truck covered with Confederate flags. Watch out for a person who thinks about money day in and day out, or one who yells obscenities at umpires. Do you agree with me that often it is clear from appearances that person X will *not* make a good mate?

I would like to see a great movie made that focuses on the abuse of a husband by a wife. I have seen this type of tragedy occur with a married couple I know. The husband has been psychologically abused for decades, and his self-confidence has been destroyed to the point that he is almost incapable of asserting himself in any way. This destruction of the ego occurs regularly as a result of abuse by a lover.

In *Ladybird, Ladybird*, an expert says of Maggie, "Her choice of a partner is in her control." Is that statement true? A close acquaintance, who suffered through an abusive relationship, shared the following with me: "You are regularly told how worthless you are, so you begin to believe that you *are* worthless and you will never be wanted by anyone worthwhile." This results in the victim giving up and remaining in the abusive relationship. Is it possible Maggie cannot spot a male who would be good for her — at least until Jorge comes along — because (a) of the childhood experience of seeing her mother abused, and (b) because she has been led to feel she is worthless?

2. Maggie loves her children. Given the evidence the experts possess, were they right to take away her children? Even when Maggie is somewhat placid, she will say things like, "Stick a bomb up his ass and it still wouldn't move him," as her way of explaining that Jorge would not desert her. Considering her history, does such language give the experts reason to think she would not be a good mother? Jorge is right when he tells social workers that what they see when Maggie erupts is "pain"— not something that would lead Maggie to become violent towards her children. Should the experts have seen what Jorge saw?

Movie 53: *If These Walls Could Talk — Part I*

Directors: Nancy Savoca, Cher; 1 hour, 37 minutes; 1996

Each of the parts of *If These Walls Could Talk* contains three episodes. Part I deals with the issue of abortion.

Part I, Episode 1: Demi Moore stars in this episode. You will be shocked and sometimes find it extremely difficult to watch. The topic is abortion. The year: 1952, a time when all abortions are illegal in the United States.

Watch Episode 1.

A question for Episode 1:

After watching this episode, ask yourself— regardless of whether you are for or against abortion — did what you see modify your view in any way? What should Claire Donnelly (Demi Moore) have done in her situation?

An essay that would be rewarding to read after watching Episode 1 is: Judith Jarvis Thomson, "A Defense of Abortion," *Philosophy and Public Affairs*, Vol. I, No. I [Fall 1971], pp. 47–66. (Also found in numerous readings texts on contemporary moral issues.)

This landmark essay has caused a lot of controversy. It contains a famous example of a kidnapped violinist, an example that has been discussed in countless university Ethics courses. Whether you like the essay or hate it, you won't forget it. Likewise, for better or worse, Episode 1 will stay with you. Demi Moore's acting is stunning and extremely courageous.

Episode 2 stars Sissy Spacek. The time is 1974. Though not as powerful as Episode 1, the characterizations are very realistic. Again the topic is abortion, and this episode provides a good follow-up to Episode 1.

Watch Episode 2.

A question for Episode 2:

Do you think Barbara Barrows (Sissy Spacek) had an easier decision to make than Claire Donnelly from Episode 1? Why or why not? Why do you think Barbara made the decision she made?

Episode 3 stars Anne Heche. The time is 1996. Cher directed this episode and plays a crucial role in it. This episode contains scenes that some people may find disturbing.

Demi Moore in an episode of *If These Walls Could Talk — Part I* (1996).

Watch Episode 3.

A question for Episode 3:

Do you think the protestors outside the abortion clinic were portrayed fairly? Christine Cullen (Anne Heche) "made a mistake" and decides to have an abortion. She needs support. Christine's friend, Patti (Jada Pinkett-Smith), is opposed to abortion, but is moved to provide the support Christine needs. Does this decision show that there are times you should do something "wrong" because it is the "right" thing to do? Why do you think Patti decided to help Christine?

Movie 54: *Real Women Have Curves*

Director: Patricia Cardoso; 1 hour, 36 minutes; 2002
Watch the movie.

Questions to ponder:

1. In *Billy Elliot* (Movie 21), Billy's father and brother were stuck in a life of working in the mines. In *Real Women Have Curves*, Ana (America Ferrera) does not want to spend her life working in the sweat shop that has trapped both her mother, Carmen (Lupe Ontiveros), and sister, Estela (Ingrid Oliu). Ana has to face the following obstacles that keep her from becoming the woman she wants to be:

   a. She's a member of a minority group.
   b. Ana's father (Jorge Cervera, Jr.) and her mother believe that families should not be broken up by members attending distant colleges. ("We are a family and we intend to stay that way.")
   c. She has an inferiority complex concerning her weight. She finally rebels against that complex when she says, "My weight says to everybody, 'Fuck you!'.... How does anyone tell me what I should look like or what I should be when there is so much more to me than my weight?" Notice that Ana is implying she is rebelling against any judgment that she is *essentially* a "fat person." Such a judgment implies "Essence precedes existence." (See Chapter 4: Anxiety and Inauthenticity.)
   d. She must find a way around those "in control," like the successful businesswoman who owns Estela's sweat shop.
   e. She has to rebel against her mother's need for Ana to be her "little baby." ("I'm not your baby anymore!")

One by one, go over the above obstacles and ask the question: How does Ana overcome obstacle A? obstacle B?, etc.

2. Ana's mother tells her to "walk like a lady" because Ana slouches as she walks. Does Ana's mother "walk like a lady"? In the last scene, Ana walks down Times Square in New York City with great confidence. Is she *then* "walking like a lady" the way her mother intended her to walk? Why couldn't her mother see that Ana could not walk with confidence unless she achieved some lifestyle like the one she lives in New York?

3. What is the significance of Ana seeing the big scar on her mother's belly?

Ana (America Ferrera), with her father Raul (Jorge Cervera, Jr.), in *Real Women Have Curves* (2002).

Movie 55: *Artemisia*

Director: Agnes Merlet; 1 hour, 36 minutes; 1997
Warning: Contains explicit sex, frontal nudity.
Artemisia is a highly fictionalized version of the apprenticeship of Artemisia Gentileschi (Valentina Cervi), daughter of the great Italian

Yahn Tregouet (left) and Valentina Cervi (right) in *Artemisia* (1997).

artist Orazio Gentileschi (Michel Serrault), to Agostino Tassi (Miki Manojlovic). The time: the early 17th century. The best biography of Artemisia is Mary D. Garrard's *Artemisia Gentileschi* (Princeton: Princeton University Press, 1991; a reprint of Garrard's 1989 work). Read that book to correct misconceptions you may pick up from the film.

Watch the movie.

Questions to ponder:

1. It is true that Orazio permitted his daughter to be tutored by Tassi, under the supervision of a chaperone. In 1612, Orazio accused Tassi of raping his daughter. In the film, Artemisia's loss of virginity does not seem to be portrayed as a result of rape. Do you agree? Also, the viewer is led to judge that Artemisia loves Tassi. If the real Artemisia was raped, should the viewer be outraged by the film? In early 17th century Italy the distinction between seduction and rape was not clearly drawn, and perhaps Tassi seduced Artemisia; should the viewer still be outraged? In recent American history, a powerful political figure engaged in some type of close physical activity with a young intern. In a sense, Artemisia was

Tassi's intern. If we are disturbed by one of these two cases, should we also be disturbed by the other?

2. I recently saw a copy of the painting "Adam and Eve" by Suzanne Valadon (1865–1938). There is Eve in all her naked glory, but Adam's interesting parts are covered by leaves. Artemisia shocks her contemporaries because she draws nude males. Clearly a double standard existed. During Artemisia's time, in Italy it was acceptable for a male to paint nude women, but women were not to paint nude males. What could be the explanation for this double standard? Is the male body obscene, but the female's is not? What exactly is beautiful about the human body that makes it the subject of so much art? If human beings had evolved to have pig-like bodies, would we judge those bodies to be beautiful? Of course, Artemisia also challenged another double standard — that men could be artists, but women could not.

Movie 56: *Whale Rider*

Director: Niki Caro; 1 hour, 45 minutes; 2002

Keisha Castle-Hughes shines in New Zealand's *Whale Rider*. Castle-Hughes plays Pai, a young Maori girl who has a dream (à la *Billy Elliot* [Movie 21]. No, she does not want to become a ballet dancer. She wants to be the leader of her tribe, a position that tradition says can only be held by males.

The message of *Whale Rider* has universal appeal, but it is refreshing seeing a movie that centers on a culture much different from our own. For the same reason, I enjoyed *Smoke Signals* (1998), a pleasant movie produced completely by Native Americans. Another excellent film on contemporary Maori culture is *Once Were Warriors* (1995), a movie that presents a dark view of the current state of that culture.

Watch the movie.

Questions to ponder:

1. Pai possesses all the characteristics necessary to be a future leader of her Maori tribe, except that she is not male. Her grandfather, Kow (Rawiri Paratene), is distraught at not being able to find anyone worthy of being a leader. He loves Pai. Why can't he see she is the one he should promote? Because of tradition? Why does tradition have such a binding effect? Think about any young girls you know. Can you spot in them

Keisha Castle-Hughes in *Whale Rider* (2003).

any sign of a potential that present tradition is stymieing? Is there anything you should do to help them reach their potential?

2. Pai's strength of character shows again and again. The two most moving scenes that capture that strength are the ones in which she gives her speech and in which she rides the whale. Beside strength of character, what other characteristics qualified her to become leader of the tribe?

Movie 57: *Daughters of the Dust*

Director: Julie Dash; 1 hour, 53 minutes; 1991

I almost left *Daughters of the Dust* out of this book. The sound on the DVD is muffled. Nearly the entire film takes place on one beach, as if characters did not have homes to go to. There seems to be little plot. I decided to include the film because of the effect it had on several female students who had previously viewed it; because it is filled with beauti-

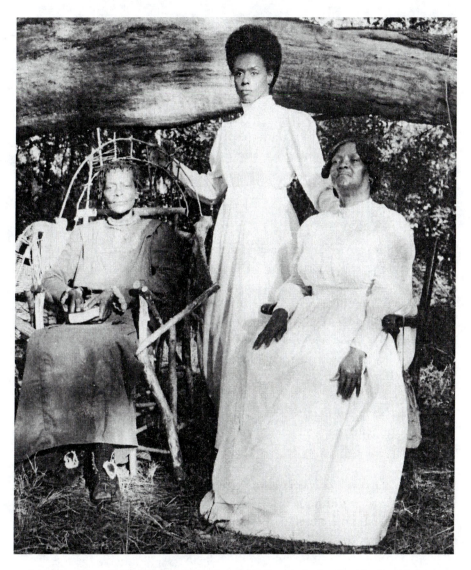

Cora Lee Day (left), Kaycee Moore (middle) and Catherine Traver (right) as members of the Peazant family in *Daughters of the Dust* (1991).

ful images; and because it is refreshing seeing a film directed by a woman who has a lot to say about descendents of African slaves living on islands off the coast of Georgia and South Carolina, particularly about the women of those communities. Though clearly produced on a low budget, *Daughters of the Dust* can move the viewer like some wonderfully written short stories that contain clearly defined characters, but which, on the surface, do not appear to have much depth.

Watch the movie.

Questions to Ponder:

1. Nana Peazant (Cora Lee Day) attempts to keep the family together by constantly reminding its members that the "ancestors" are always present and, if the living make the effort, the wisdom of the ancestors will make itself known. She says that even the baby in the womb is one with the ancestors. She uses this idea to try to pacify Eli Peazant (Adisa Anderson), whose wife Eula (Alva Rogers) is pregnant as the result of rape. Nana says to Eli, "We carry these memories inside of we…. I'm tryin' to learn ya how to touch your own spirit…. I'm tryin' to give ya somethin' to take north with ya…. Count on those old Africans, Eli. They come to ya when ya least expect them." It is difficult for Eli to keep from rejecting his violated wife. Is there anything in Nana's argument that Eli should accept as a remedy to his mental suffering? Is there any sense to be made of Nana's claim to Eli that he doesn't have to worry about the baby Eula carries not being his? According to Nana, it doesn't matter how the unborn child was conceived because that child is one with the ancestors.

2. Nana not only stresses that the deeds of ancestors have an effect on the present, but that what present members of the family do will have a tremendous influence on descendents, "not today, not tomorrow, will come the reapin' of the true deeds we do but in some for-veiled and mighty harvest." Is Nana's lesson that what we do in our lives will find its "harvest" in future generations something all human beings should accept? Would there necessarily be more caring in the world if we all were more concerned about future generations than we generally seem to be?

3. Nana tells Eli he *married* Eula, he doesn't *own* her. That is a distinction many more men should learn. How would you clarify the difference between "being married to person A" and "owning person A"?

ADDITIONAL RECOMMENDATIONS
FOR FILMS DEALING WITH SEXISM

Personal Velocity (2002). Rebecca Miller's directional debut is actually three short movies based on stories published in Miller's book of the same name. In *Personal Velocity*, you will meet Delia (Kyra Sedgwick), Greta (Parker Posey) and Paula (Fairuza Balk), three ordinary women who are at a stage in their lives when they must decide the course of their future.

Oleanna (1994). A David Mamet masterpiece. He is also the writer-director of Movie 3, *House of Games*. Here Mamet addresses the breakdown of communication between a college professor (William H. Macy) and one of his female students (Debra Eisenstadt). Is the professor guilty of sexual harassment? If not, will he be able to adequately defend himself?

Nine to Five (1980). A light movie with a serious theme. Too many women in the workplace are treated like pieces of— for lack of a better word — furniture. Three women (Jane Fonda, Dolly Parton and Lily Tomlin) aim to put their boss (Dabney Coleman) in his place.

14

Gay Rights

Some years ago, the actress Shirley MacLaine said that as she got older she cared less and less about who was sleeping with whom. I've experienced that same transition myself.

A person's sexual preference depends on the desire that comes to the person when faced with another person who, often unknowingly, stimulates that desire. That such a desire suddenly arises is neither rational nor the result of free choice. The desire merely arises as an effect of past genetic and physiological programming. For the life of me, I sometimes can't see how Person A is attracted to Person B. I wouldn't kiss Person B if someone gave me $100; I'd throw up! (One thousand dollars would probably be acceptable, however.) For whatever reason, Person A feels desire for Person B. A kiss from Person B would be "heaven" for Person A.

Though the above is an inadequate, rough outline of the reasons behind sexual love, the mechanisms that trigger desire work much the same, whether in heterosexual or homosexual relationships. On what grounds should homosexual desire be condemned? Various philosophers have attempted to show that homosexual acts are immoral because:

A. They are "unnatural."

B. Homosexuals are really sexually frustrated, unhappy individuals who have serious problems dealing with members of the opposite sex. If homosexuals would reach a point where they had a healthy sexual relationship with a member of the opposite sex, they would be happier and realize they had been miserable when they were engaged in any homosexual relationship.

C. It is important to preserve and protect the traditional family, and homosexuality tends to damage that tradition.

The problem is that each of the above reasons given in criticism of homosexuality contains serious weaknesses. A, for example, fails to establish the premise that "everything 'unnatural' is bad." Is penicillin "natural"? I would have died long ago if scientists had not invented "unnatural" medicines that kept me alive. Not only are some "unnatural" things good, but some "natural" things are not good. Male domination of the female can be viewed as "natural."

Concerning B, think of all the unhappiness found in so many heterosexual relationships. There is widespread abuse and lack of communication in such relationships. Think of the divorce rate. Are homosexuals more sexually "frustrated" than heterosexuals?

Concerning C, how does the acceptance of the fact that some persons *naturally* desire persons of their own sex damage the traditional family? There are enough people who desire members of the opposite sex to keep that tradition alive.

On utilitarian grounds there seems little justification for viewing homosexuality as immoral. Jeremy Bentham, the founder of Utilitarianism, wrote an amazing essay on homosexuality in the late 18th century. He analyzed various objections against homosexuals and reached the following conclusion: "I have been tormented myself for years to find if possible a sufficient ground for treating [homosexuals] with the severity with which they are treated at this time of day by all European nations; but upon the principle of utility I can find none."[1]

Movie 58: *Chasing Amy*

Director: Kevin Smith; 1 hour, 53 minutes; 1997

Warning: Even though *Chasing Amy* does not contain explicit scenes of sexual activity, the language and the content of conversations could be very disturbing to some people.

Watch the movie.

Questions to ponder:

1. A central issue for Holden (Ben Affleck) is whether a woman is a virgin if she has not had sex with a male, but *has* had sex with another female. In the movie, the following possible definitions of the phrase "a female's loss of virginity" are given: (a) "has had intercourse with a mem-

Ben Affleck (left) and Joey Lauren Adams (right) in *Chasing Amy* (1997).

ber of the opposite sex," (b) "when you've made love for the first time" with a member of your own sex or with a member of the opposite sex, (c) "when the hymen is broken," (d) "when there is physical penetration by a penis," (e) "when there is physical penetration by a bodily part other than a penis," (f) "when there is emotional penetration." Which of the above "definitions" do you accept or reject? Why?

2. Holden does not accept Alyssa (Joey Lauren Adams) for what she is, but sees her as he wants her to be. Is that love? He expects her to "adjust." How does one adjust one's sexual orientation?

3. Holden doesn't much mind that Alyssa has had sex with females, but it drives him nuts when he finds out she had sex with males. Is that strange? After all, the pleasure she would have obtained in her relations with women may have been more satisfying than that in her relations with men. In the scene outside the hockey rink — a powerful scene that merits re-watching — Alyssa asks, "Do you mean to tell me that while you have zero problems with me sleeping with half the women in New York City, you have some sort of half-assed, mealy-mouthed objection

to sex I had with guys almost ten years ago?" What, if any, problems do you have with Alyssa's sexual history?

4. Given the fact that Alyssa truly loves Holden, what relevance is there to her past sexual experiences? (Just think of how many relationships are fractured by this issue!) Holden says, "I feel inadequate 'cause you've had such a big life and so much experience. And my life's been pretty small in comparison." She answers, "That doesn't matter to me." In those past experiences she didn't find what she was looking for; she found it in Holden. Should Holden see that Alyssa's response is adequate?

5. In the audio commentary included on the DVD, there is a statement by the director, Kevin Smith, that Holden wants Alyssa to apologize for her life before she met him. Are there any conditions under which such a desire would be reasonable? Does the present love cancel out all the undesirable facts about a loved one's pre-relationship life?

Movie 59: *If These Walls Could Talk — Part II*

Directors: Jane Anderson, Martha Coolidge, Anne Heche; 1 hour, 36 minutes; 2000

Each of the parts of *If These Walls Could Talk* contains three episodes. Part II centers on dilemmas faced by lesbians.

Watch Episode 1. The year is 1961.

Questions for Episode 1:

My questions for this episode are for people who think gays should not be granted the rights heterosexuals have.

Edith (Vanessa Redgrave) and Abby (Marian Seldes) have been companions and lovers for 50 years. Photographs of the couple show the love they shared over the decades. The episode wonderfully captures Edith's unspeakable grief as she returns alone to the home she and Abby shared. Her grief is no less than that of a heterosexual who loses his or her spouse. Given those facts, on what grounds would Abby's relatives have a greater right to the house and all contained in it than Edith? Doesn't Edith have the right to know what is occurring while Abby is dying in the hospital? If you agree that the home is obviously Edith's and Edith did have a right to be informed while in the hospital, should you not agree that same-sex marriages should be honored so that cases like Edith's will not occur?

Watch Episode 2. The year is 1972.

A question for Episode 2:
    The following key quote from this episode is uttered by Linda (Michelle Williams): "Do you know why you don't like Amy? It's because you're scared of anyone who is not like you." She is addressing her lesbian friends because they reject her "boyfriend" (Chloe Sevigny), a female transvestite. If *you* are opposed to lesbian relationships, is it "because you're scared of anyone who is not like you"?
    Watch Episode 3. The year is 2000.

Questions for Episode 3:
    Should Fran (Sharon Stone) and Kal (Ellen DeGeneris) be permitted to parent a child? Would the case be different if the two persons involved were not fictional characters, but rather the real Sharon Stone and Ellen DeGeneris (two wealthy, intelligent, highly admired women)?

Sharon Stone (left) and Ellen DeGeneris (right) in an episode of *If These Walls Could Talk — Part II* (2000).

Movie 60: *Philadelphia*

Director: Jonathan Demme; 2 hours, 5 minutes; 1993
Watch the movie.

Questions to ponder:

    1. Did the movie convince you that people like Andrew Beckett (Tom Hanks) should not be fired from their jobs because they are gay or because they have AIDS? Why or why not? Why should anyone judge other people's sexual preferences as long as their sexual behavior does not affect their job performance?
    2. Suppose the movie were about a young gay boy who wants to

Attorney Joe Miller (Denzel Washington, right) represents Andrew Beckett (Tom Hanks, left) in *Philadelphia* (1997).

join the Boy Scouts. Should the boy be accepted into the Scouts ? Why or why not?

3. Should there be any restrictions on gays joining the military? Why or why not?

Movie 61: *The Celluloid Closet*

Directors: Rob Epstein and Jeffrey Friedman; 1 hour; 41 minutes; 1995

Watch the movie.

Questions to ponder:

1. In the film, Quentin Crisp points out that when a woman like Greta Garbo dresses like a man, she is judged to be sexy. When a man

**Two men dance together in an 1895 experimental film featured in *The Cellu-
loid Closet* (1995).**

dresses like a woman, most of the audience will laugh. Why do people
react that way?

   2. Stewart Stern, the screenwriter of *Rebel Without a Cause* said that,
contrary to popular belief, the relationship between the characters played
by James Dean and Sal Mineo was not intended to be a homosexual relationship. At the same time, he says, any film is "an offering to an audience to create their own film." I disagree with his latter statement. If he
who created the characters did not create them as being in a homosexual relationship, then a viewer who judges they *are* in a homosexual relationship is perhaps reading an untruth into the film. People of the same
sex can show affection for each other and not be homosexuals. A gay person can show affection for a heterosexual person and not be heterosexual. Several of the scenes presented in *The Celluloid Closet* do not seem
to involve homosexual behavior. The scenes of Laurel and Hardy hug-
ging, and Thelma and Louise kissing, show affection but should not be

taken as proof that those characters are gay. The scene from *Philadelphia* showing Tom Hanks and Antonio Banderas dancing is another matter. Their characters are clearly lovers. Do you agree with my assessment? Why?

3. *The Celluloid Closet* traces various attempts to formulate some kind of moral code that would put restrictions on what can be shown on the movie screen. Sometimes it is some official body like the Hayes Commission that institutes rules for censorship. Sometimes it is the informal thing called "public opinion." Filmmakers want to make money and are often afraid to anger members of the audience. Therefore, watered-down versions of movies are distributed. (Notice the number of "director's cuts" that have been released on DVD and video.) As years pass, more and more people see how wrong those forces of censorship are. *The Celluloid Closet* contains interviews of people who are aware of the dangers of censorship. This documentary shows the travesty of the farcical depiction of gays in movies in the past. It shows the hurt such depictions caused gay viewers. What restrictions, if any, would *you* place on what can be shown in movies?

I accept the position given years ago by one of my professors that the censor is often more obscene than the material censored. The idea that a person may view something, but then subsequently judge that I cannot view it, is very disturbing.

ADDITIONAL RECOMMENDATIONS
FOR FILMS FOCUSING ON GAY RIGHTS

Before Night Falls (2001). Several wonderful movies about famous creative people have been released in the last few years. *Frida* (2002) and *Iris* (2001) are among the best. *Before Night Falls* is another. The film presents the life of the gay Cuban poet Reinaldo Arenas. The fine Spanish actor Javier Bardem plays Arenas. Sean Penn appears in a small role. Arenas was arrested by the Castro government because of his gay lifestyle. Johnny Depp appears in prison scenes. You'll find the role(s) played by Depp very interesting.

Show Me Love (1998). Swedish movie about Agnes, who is attracted to Elin. Girl meets girl and finally wins her over. It's not easy. Elin is the most popular girl in her school. The town of Amal is not going to look favorably on their relationship. Some fluff, but the last scene is memorable.

Hedwig and the Angry Inch (2001). Comedy/Rock Musical. Hansel (John Cameron Mitchell) undergoes a botched sex change operation. As a result, she becomes Hedwig and performs in a band called "The Angry Inch." Great music. In the midst of the comedy and music is a serious story about the search for completeness — finding another person who will "complete" you, making you feel like a "complete human being." The movie won the Audience Award at the 2001 Sundance Festival.

Bedrooms and Hallways (1998). A British comedy. Leo (Kevin McKidd) can't get a date, so he joins a club for straight men and becomes attracted to every member of the group.

The Adventures of Priscilla, Queen of the Desert (1994). An Australian comedy. These actors give amazing performances: Guy Pearce, who also stars in *Memento* (Movie 73); Hugo Weaving, who also appears as Agent Smith in *The Matrix* (Movie 24); and Terence Stamp, who is excellent in *The Limey* (1999). Weaving and Pearce are drag queens, and Stamp is a transsexual. The three go on a road trip into the Australian Outback to give lip-synch performances in various towns.

Boys Don't Cry (1999): Based on a true story about a guy named Brandon Teena (Hilary Swank) who is biologically a girl, Teena Brandon. Why Brandon is attracted to scumbag rednecks who will lead to his/her downfall is not clear, but Hilary Swank gives an awesome performance. In the movie, Swank *is* a guy. She won the Oscar for Best Actress.

Gods and Monsters (1998): Ian McKellen as elderly James Whale, gay director of the original *Frankenstein* film. Whale is attracted to a gardener (Brandon Fraser). There is more depth to the movie than may meet the eye. Gandalf shows his range as an actor.

Wilde (1998): Oscar's trials (literally) and tribulations.

I recommend *www.aboutgaymovies.info* as a source. This website contains a regularly updated list of scores of movies about gays and lesbians.

15

Pornography

Freedom of speech is limited — as it should be. We cannot yell "Fire" in a crowded building when there is no fire and then claim we were merely exercising our right to free speech. The question is not, "Should *any* speech be prohibited?" but rather, "*What* speech should be prohibited?" The two films in this chapter center on the issue of pornography and censorship. "What is 'pornographic'?" and "What material — if any — that is considered pornographic should be censored?" are the more specific questions concerning free speech that are addressed in these movies.

No reasonable person disagrees that child pornography is immoral and should be illegal because, among other reasons, it distorts children's sexuality before their natural maturity. However, there is far greater disagreement about a film discussed in Chapter 16 entitled *The Lover* (Movie 66). If that movie were shown to the general public, many would judge it to be "filth." Others, including this author — and I hope all my readers — would judge *The Lover* to be an amazingly beautiful work of art.

I will not go into detail about attempts to define "pornography." Basically, I accept the view that a pornographic work is one created for the sole purpose of sexually arousing the person perusing it. Someone can watch *The Lover* in order to become sexually aroused, but that was not the sole purpose of the explicit scenes in the movie. Likewise, someone who is easily offended might view *The Lover* and only see explicit sexual acts. (One of my closest relatives will judge a film obscene if it contains the word "damn" in it.)

Though my reasoning involves some circularity, I hold that a central element of pornographic movies is that they are boring. Years ago, while I was preparing to teach a course entitled "Philosophies of Love and Sexuality," I decided to check out porno shops while in San Francisco for a conference. After all, one of the standard topics in such a course is "pornography," and I didn't want to cover the topic without firsthand knowledge of pornographic material. So I entered a porno shop. There were all kinds of gadgets for sale. Magazines filled the racks. In a back room there were short films that could be viewed for 25 cents each. I started watching a movie. At that point I realized I had entered a *gay* porno shop. (That explains why some guys looked at me the way they did when I entered the shop; I was pretty handsome back in those days.) Despite the fact that my sexual preference was not theirs, my research was certainly going well.

After leaving that shop, I decided I should also visit a porno shop for heterosexuals. I found one down the street and entered. The same types of gadgets were on sale. I went into the back room and watched a few films. Boy, were they boring! The acting stank. Did I believe the "actors" and "actresses" were really having orgasms? No! In addition, there was no plot worth mentioning. The cameraman, or camerawoman, had to have a *very* small camera because there were scenes showing penis-entering-vagina from mere inches away. It looked like pistons pumping up and down. *Boring!* Those people who think pornography will cause a viewer to become a sexual pervert have it wrong. If anyone becomes a sexual pervert after viewing what I saw, he or she has problems caused by previous conditions — conditions that do not impact me. Watching pornography is torture to me — because it's so dull! I wouldn't become a pervert — I'd fall asleep.

Movie 62: *The People vs. Larry Flynt*

Director: Milos Forman; 2 hours, 10 minutes; 1996
Watch the movie.

Questions to ponder:

1. Larry (Woody Harrelson) says, "All I'm guilty of is bad taste." Is he "guilty" of anything else other than bad taste because of his publishing explicit sexual pictures? Was the Supreme Court wrong to rule in Larry's favor on the Jerry Falwell issue? Jerry Falwell does not come across well in this film or in *The Eyes of Tammy Faye* (Movie 19).

2. Alan Isaacman (Edward Norton) argues that, "We live in a free country.... But there is a price for that freedom which is that sometimes we have to tolerate things that we don't necessarily like." Is that a good argument for supporting Larry Flynt's publication? We have to tolerate

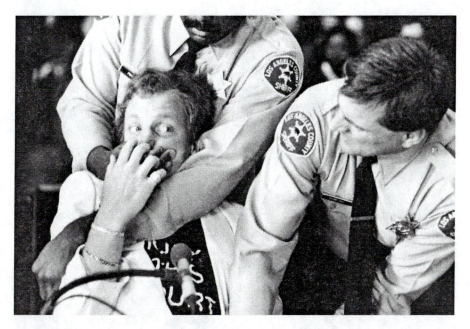

A judge orders sheriff's deputies to gag Larry (Woody Harrelson) in *The People vs. Larry Flynt* (1996).

religions we may not agree with because of the right to freedom of religion, but there are limits to that right. If a religion arises that practices torturing children, that practice would be stopped.

3. At one point in the movie, Alan uses the "domino effect argument." If you silence Larry Flynt, then later it will be okay to silence other people who are not as outrageous as Flynt. "If we start throwing up walls against what some of us think is obscene, we may very well wake up one morning and realize that walls have been thrown up in all kinds of places that we never expected ... and that's not freedom." Larry Flynt offends some people. *Huckleberry Finn* offends others. Shakespeare offends others. The Bible offends some. Are you afraid of the domino effect?

4. What is your reaction to Flynt's speech during which he shows photos and implies there are many things that are more obscene than photos of sexual acts, but those things can legally be published? Are photos of Ku Klux Klanners more — or less — obscene than photos of sex acts? Is a photo of a penis or vagina more obscene than a photo of someone's beer belly hanging out over his pants? Why?

Michael DeGood as *The Pornographer* (1999).

Movie 63: *The Pornographer*

Director: Doug Atchison; 1 hour, 28 minutes; 1999

Initially, I was going to use *Boogie Nights* (1997) in this slot. However, I think the low-budget film *The Pornographer* is a bit more thought-provoking than that better known movie. I recommend watching both and comparing them. Both, for example, include scenes about awards for best porn and mention the fantasy held by some porn-makers that they are creating some *high-quality* material.

In *Boogie Nights*, Burt Reynolds gives an outstanding performance as an almost likable porn producer-director. Most of the "actors" and "actresses" in his movies seem to be healthy and to love their work. *The Pornographer*, on the other hand, presents the porn industry at its sleazy worst. Craig Wasson is excellent as Spano, a very unlikable producer of porn. Since it is a realistic portrayal of a nasty industry, be warned: *The Pornographer* is not a Walt Disney movie. However, at the same time, it is not as explicit as it appears to be. There are scenes in which sex acts are performed — under covers. *That* fakery drives me nuts. Whenever I see such scenes — and they are common — I know the filmmakers have chickened out. They are afraid of an NC–17 rating. The truth is: *No one has sexual relations under covers!* The covers get in the way! Such scenes are almost as bad as the famous lovemaking scene on the beach in *From Here to Eternity*. HA! Try making love on a sandy beach. The sand will act like sandpaper! Plus, even in a scene in *The Pornographer* where covers are used to hide private parts, I swear I saw a bit of the female's panties! I kid you not. Look for it. Try making love with panties on!

Watch the movie.

Questions to ponder:

1. In his commentary that accompanies the DVD, Doug Atchison, the writer and director, states the movie is about love, not porn. Do you agree? Why?

2. By the end of the movie, is Paul (Michael DeGood) cured of his addiction to porn? If so, what cured him?

3. A standard objection to porn is presented by Paul's co-worker, Teresa (Marjorie Harris). Porn, she says, is the ultimate degradation of women. She says to Paul:

> "Is that how you see women? Purely as sex objects, things to be objectified, and pursued and conquered? ... There's sick people out there. They watch this stuff and use it to justify the things they do ... the way they treat women, abuse women, rape women.... You are showing sex cut off from any lasting human emotion..."

Theresa goes on to claim that most women in porn come from broken homes and have been sexually abused when young. In his commentary, Doug Atchison makes similar claims. He is not against watching porn, but "the people who are in porn are real human beings that we are using for our own pleasure, and a lot of them have problems, a lot of them come from very troubled backgrounds." If it is true that (a) porn degrades women *and* (b) many actresses in pornographic movies have "troubled backgrounds," is there sufficient reason to ban such movies?

Comments:

Concerning question 2 above, it is clear Paul is cured. An interesting comparison could be made between the curing of porn addiction in this film and the curing of Alex's violent tendency in *A Clockwork Orange*

(1971). Alex is cured when forced to watch filmed acts of violence while listening to works of Beethoven, the composer he idolizes. When porn is connected to the one female who shows him respect, Paul rebels against it.

ADDITIONAL RECOMMENDATIONS
FOR FILMS DEALING WITH PORNOGRAPHY

Quills (2000). Geoffrey Rush's best role since he won the Oscar for *Shine* (1996). Here he plays the Marquis de Sade. Excellent plot, but I am not crazy about the casting of Jaoquin Phoenix as an abbé, Michael Caine as the person charged with controlling de Sade, or Kate Winslet as de Sade's helpmate.

Boogie Nights (1997). The rise and fall of Eddie Adams (Mark Wahlberg), alias "Dirk Diggler," porn star. Burt Reynolds is memorable as Jack Horner, a producer of porno movies.

16

Love, Love, Love

"Philosophies of Love," a very non-traditional course, has become popular on many college campuses in the last 30 years. Many of us think we know what love is. Philosophers, however, have stressed the multiplicity of *types* of love. Comradeship, for example, is a form of love. Comradeship is captured in *Saving Private Ryan* (Movie 37). In this chapter, other forms of love are presented. In *When Harry Met Sally*, friendship between male and female is addressed. *East-West* is a movie that centers on the love of a spouse. An adulterous love affair is the topic of *The Bridges of Madison County*. *Babette's Feast*—one of my all-time favorite movies—is clearly about love, but is not a standard love story involving sexual love or parental love; the love in *Babette's Feast* can be seen as something similar to *agape* (Christian love). *Pop and Me* is a wonderful documentary about the relationship between father and son.

Clearly, a number of movies from other chapters also center on love. They include the love of the land felt by Bull McCabe in *The Field*. An excellent presentation of Christian love can be found in *Dead Man Walking*. Romantic and sexual love are central themes in *Hannah and Her Sisters*, *Tess*, *Sliding Doors*, *Under the Sand* and *Chasing Amy*. In fact, probably the majority of films made involve significant portions dedicated to one form of love or another. Why? Because love is one of the most important—and dramatic—realities to us. In my view, everyone wants to love and be loved. Films give us scenes of love that, in some ways, for a few moments, make us feel that *we* are experiencing that love first-hand.

Movie 64: *When Harry Met Sally*

Director: Rob Reiner; 1 hour, 36 minutes; 1989

> "A dog is man's best friend."
> "You've got a friend in Pennsylvania."

"A friend in need is a friend indeed."
"What a friend we have in Jesus."

Above are just a few of the sayings you've all heard about friends. (Think about the "friend in need" one. What does it mean? It seems it should say: "I'll be a friend when you're in need." But no! The friend *in need* is the friend indeed!?)

What is a friend? The best answer to that question was provided over 2000 years ago by the great philosopher Aristotle. Most of what he said about the nature of friendship still holds true after all this time. A central notion in Aristotle's analysis of friendship is that true friends are *good* for each other. A "friend" who leads friends to do evil is not a friend. It follows that the members of Charlie Manson's "family" were *not* friends, though they would claim they were. As Aristotle put it, "Perfect friendship is the friendship of men who are good."[1] Such friendships tend to last longer than friendships based on pleasure or usefulness. Since truly good people are rare, it follows that "perfect" friendships are rare. Of course, perfect friends give pleasure to one another and are useful to each other.

Aristotle stresses friendship between men. He does not seem capable of seeing that women, too, can be good, noble, temperate, and capable of the highest intellectual activities and thus can be worthy friends. He clearly would not have had time for the friendship presented in *When Harry Met Sally*— the friendship between an adult male and an adult female. In the movie, Harry (Billy Crystal) tells Sally (Meg Ryan), "Men and women can't be friends because the sex part always gets in the way." Though Aristotle never specifically addresses the possibility of men and women being friends, it is clear he would agree with Harry. Do *you* agree with Harry?

Watch the movie.

Questions to ponder:

1. Suppose male X and female Y have lovers or spouses. Can X and Y be friends? Harry says, "That doesn't work ... because ... the person you are involved with can't understand why you need to be friends with the person you're just friends with. Like it means something is missing from the relationship and you have to go outside the relationship to get it." Can there be an exception to Harry's rule?

Sally (Meg Ryan) and Harry (Billy Crystal) in *When Harry Met Sally*.

2. The scene in the restaurant where Meg Ryan fakes an orgasm is very famous. Men — you might ask yourself whether or not you can ever know if your mate is faking it. "She is not faking" is a synthetic sentence (see Chapter 1 — Did You Ever Think You Knew Something but You Didn't?). Wow, this topic is depressing, fellas!

3. Both Harry and Sally have had a number of close relationships with people of the opposite sex. What was it that — years after they first met — "clicked" for them? What led them to become friends? What did they see in each other that finally led them to become lovers?

Movie 65: *East-West*

Director: Regis Wargnier; 2 hours, 5 minutes; 1999
Watch the movie.

Questions to ponder:

1. Alexei (Oleg Menshikov) and Marie (Sandrine Bonnaire) love one another when they arrive in Russia with their son after World War II. Immediately after disembarking, the reality of Stalinist Russia hits them

Catherine Deneuve (left), Sandrine Bonnaire (middle) and Erwan Baynaud (right) in *East-West* (1999).

full force. In the months that follow, Marie rejects Alexei and takes on Sacha (Sergei Bodrov, Jr.) as a lover. Why does she reject Alexei and why was she attracted to Sacha? What was it about Marie that attracts Sacha?

2. Early in their life in Russia, Alexei says to Marie, "What I miss most is having you to myself. Being totally free and you looking so beautiful. The two of us together alone in the world." They live in a crowded apartment. Spies are everywhere. There is no political freedom. Do such conditions undermine the stability of a love relationship? Will love thrive better in a society in which there is the ability to be alone and in which people are free? (Think of the divorce rate in the United States.)

3. Alexei is banished to a Pacific Island and does not get to leave Russia for 30 years. Out of his love for Marie and their son, he sacrifices his own happiness. Should Marie have stayed with him? Why, or why not?

If you liked *East-West*, try *Indochine* (1992) and *The Thief* (1997). *Indochine* is directed by Regis Wargnier who is the director of *East-West*. Catherine Deneuve, who plays the French actress who helps Marie in *East-West*, plays the lead in *Indochine*. *The Thief*, written and directed by Pavel Chukhraj, contains scenes of life in overcrowded apartment complexes in the post-war Stalinist era, very similar to those scenes in *East-West*. The plot of *The Thief* is every bit as original as that of *East-West*. Misha Philipchuk gives one of the most mesmerizing performances I've ever seen from a child actor.

Movie 66: *The Lover*

Director: Jean-Jacques Annaud; 1 hour, 55 minutes; 1992
Warning: Contains explicit sexual scenes. Never has sex on film been so artistic. Personally, I never thought sex could be so beautiful.
The Lover is based on Marguerite Duras' memoir of the same title. Watch the movie.

Questions to ponder:

1. Did the young girl (Jane March) love the Chinese man (Tony Leung) during the time they shared the Bachelor's Room? If so, why does she say such nasty things to him, such as, "I have no love for you," and, "I cared only about the money?" If part of the answer is that she was so

Tony Leung approaches Jane March on a ferry crossing the Mekong in *The Lover* (1992).

young, then should she have been in the relationship in the first place? *Was* she too young?

2. What drew the Chinese man to the young girl? Her beauty? (The way she stands with one leg up on a railing of a ship with her loose dress and captivating hat certainly attracts the viewer's attention!) It is clear he loved her with a love that is not just sexual. In the last scene we find out that the love he felt was life-long. Is it impossible to explain the grounds for such a love? Plato said love is a "divine madness." Does that label fit the love of the Chinese man?

3. The Chinese man says, "Before you, I knew nothing about suffering." He says that in part because of the way she treats him. He could also say it because in his culture he is not permitted to marry her. But does love always carry with it a type and depth of suffering not experienced in other relationships? It certainly does when a loved one dies (see *Shadowlands*, Movie 28). But I am asking about suffering that exists on a day-to-day basis while one is in a living relationship.

Movie 67: *The Bridges of Madison County*

Director: Clint Eastwood; 2 hours, 15 minutes; 1995
Watch the movie.

Questions to ponder:

1. In her letter to her children, Francesca (Meryl Streep) asks if anyone else could "see the beauty" of her affair with Robert (Clint Eastwood). Do you see that beauty? If the beauty is there, is her adulterous affair immoral? Why or why not?

2. Francesca's family life has become stale. Her husband does not fulfill her dreams. Robert is interesting. Francesca and he laugh together. The time she spends with him is fulfilling. She is happy. Robert knows how she feels. He appreciates her cooking and is helpful in the kitchen. He is basically the perfect man for Francesca. How can she pass up the chance to go with him? Immanuel Kant would say she should not go with Robert, much less have an affair with him. What would a utilitarian say? (Remember, Francesca says she was "more herself than ever before" when she was with him. In her family, she is basically a servant.)

3. Francesca says that if she leaves with Robert they'll lose their love. Why would that loss occur?

Meryl Streep and Clint Eastwood in *The Bridges of Madison County* (1995).

Movie 68: *Sidewalks of New York*

Director: Edward Burns; 1 hour, 47 minutes; 2001
Watch the movie.

Questions to ponder:

1. Annie Matthews (Heather Graham), whose husband Griffin (Stanley Tucci) is having an affair but denies it, says "almost everyone I know is just obsessed with their sexuality and their sexual life and I just think all this thinking about it can't be healthy. If you just look at the television, movies, Internet, I mean, everyone is just obsessed. They just spend all their time thinking and talking about their sexual lives.... I mean, who cares about love any more? Doesn't anyone care about that?" Is *Sidewalks of New York* itself obsessed with sexual themes? Does it present a true picture of just how many people are obsessed with sex? Which characters in the film, if any, do indeed care about love? Which characters don't?

2. Does *Sidewalks of New York* promote casual sex?

3. The voice of the person who interviews the characters in the film

Rosario Dawson (left) and Edward Burns (right) meet on the *Sidewalks of New York* (2001).

asks, "Is it love or sex that makes us so confused in our relationships?" If you grant that many people are "confused" in their close relations, is that confusion caused by love, sex, or some other factor(s)?

4. Do you think there can be love at first sight? Is there any instance of that phenomenon shown in the film? Do you think sexual relations right after love at first sight is always immoral? What about Tommy (Ed Burns) and Maria (Rosario Dawson) having sexual relations on the first date? Is this immoral?

5. As a result of her fling with Tommy, Maria becomes pregnant. Why doesn't she tell Tommy about the pregnancy when she intends to? Should she have told him?

Movie 69: *Indecent Proposal*

Director: Adrian Lyne; 1 hour, 56 minutes; 1993
Watch the movie.

Questions to ponder:

Robert Redford and Demi Moore in *Indecent Proposal* (1993).

1. Are there limits to what money can buy? If you think there are limits, give examples of things that would cross the line.

2. What do you think motivates John Gage (Robert Redford) to make his offer? Do you think he really meant the money was for one night with Diana and nothing else?

3. Most people probably think Gage's offer is immoral. Would the offer have been more or less immoral if Gage wasn't Robert Redford but an uncharismatic, pimply-faced multi-millionaire?

4. Before making the deal, should David (Woody Harrelson) and Diana (Demi Moore) have known that David would react the way he did after the night was over?

5. What do you think will unfold *after* David and Diana meet on the pier in the last scene? Will David try to pry from Diana the reason she returned to him? If he finds out she left Gage because she thinks Gage has had numerous "million dollar girls," how will he react? Will he think she would have stayed with Gage if she had been the only one?

Movie 70: *Babette's Feast*

Director: Gabriel Axel; 1 hour, 43 minutes; 1987

The movies covered thus far in this chapter have centered on romantic and sexual love. *Babette's Feast* and the next film, *Pop and Me*, center on two very different forms of love not stressed thus far. *Pop and Me* will bring up issues involving parental love. I interpret *Babette's Feast* to be a film that highlights *agape*, or Christian love. I, however, will utilize ideas from Martin Buber's *I and Thou* to give what I see as a view of love similar to, but broader than, Christian love.

As mentioned briefly in my comments on *The Decalogue* (Movie 20), Buber holds that there are two ways human beings can relate to each other and to natural things. One way he calls the "I-it" relation. If a person is in an I-it relationship, the thing being related to is just that — a thing. People, for the most part, are in I-it relationships. The pen I use in writing these words is an "it" — a mere instrument to be used. If it runs out of ink, I throw it away. No big loss.

There is another type of relationship, however. Buber calls it the "I-Thou" relationship. When a person is in an I-Thou relationship, his or her "whole being" is involved. This totality would not be the case in an I-it relationship. One discovers *depth* when confronted with a Thou. There is lack of depth in the world of things. Using a religious word, one can say that when confronted with a Thou, something "sacred" is present. In fact, Buber is clear that when there is an I-Thou relationship, God is present, since God *is* Relation.

One of my favorite quotes from all the philosophical works I've read comes from *I and Thou*. Buber claims: "All real living is meeting."[2] People who experience the I-it form of relationship are not really living! In *Babette's Feast* there is a wonderful portrayal of an evening when a small community in Denmark experiences "real life." They experience depth. They experience love. The way they talk, the way they eat, and the way they act — all indicate they have transcended the realm of mere things.

We cannot live without things. As Buber put it, "Without *It* man cannot live. But he who lives with *It* alone is not a man."[3] Things are necessary for survival. However, one is not "really living" if one is merely surviving.

Buber holds there are three "spheres" of I-Thou relationships. They are: "our life with nature," "our life with men," and "our life with spiritual beings."[4] Of the sphere of our life with nature, Buber gives examples of how we can relate to such things as trees and horses. A tree can be cut down for firewood. A horse can be used to pull a cart. They are then "things" being used. However, a tree or a horse can also be related to as a "Thou." Most of the time we gulp our food. Food is just stuff to be consumed. But Buber claims that eating should be a sacred act. In *Babette's Feast*, the people eating at the feast are not merely consuming stuff.

During the feast, love reigns. Each is a Thou for the others.

Buber's "third sphere" puzzles some people. What does it mean to have an "I-Thou" relation with "spiritual beings"? Martin Buber is not being weird here. He is not proposing there are "ghosts" or "angels" present. He gives an example which clarifies what he means:

> Let the questioner make present to himself one of the traditional sayings of a master who died thousands of years ago; and let him attempt, as well as he can, to take and receive the sayings with his ears, that is, as though spoken by the speaker in his presence, even spoken to him. To do this he must turn with his whole being to the speaker (who is not at

Stephane Audran stars as Babette in *Babette's Feast* (1987).

hand) of the saying (which is at hand). This means that he must adopt towards him who is both dead and living the attitude which I call the saying of *Thou*.[5]

In the film, the minister — who is dead — is a presence at the feast. Buber is dead — but if we open ourselves to his words, it is as if he is speaking to us.

Watch the movie.

Questions to ponder:

1. Does *Babette's Feast* prove that religious or philosophical views which denigrate all physical pleasure are misguided? (One of the minister's disciples said before the feast, "The food is of no importance.") Isn't the feast a sacred event?

2. Why does Babette (Stephane Audran) decide to stay with the sisters after winning the lottery? Why did she want to prepare the birthday meal? The sisters were satisfied with a "modest supper." Why did she want it to be a French meal?

3. Did you spot what I see as a major flaw in the film? General Lowenhielm (Jarl Kulle) is given food unlike any he has tasted since years before when he had dined at a Parisian restaurant where the chef, a woman, could "transform a dinner into a kind of love affair — a love affair that made no distinction between bodily appetite and spiritual appetite." Why wouldn't he ask to meet the cook (Babette) at the feast? Do you see this inaction as a flaw in the movie?

Movie 71: *Pop and Me*

Director: Chris Roe; 1 hour, 32 minutes; 1999

The love between parent and child is difficult to convey with words. Part of the explanation for the depth of that love must reside in the innate desire programmed into parents to protect the child for the purpose of sustaining future generations of the species. Wishing that health, prosperity and happiness be the lot of the child is a central element of the love felt by the parent. When it turns out that a child does not possess one of these "goods," the parent is wracked with guilt and despair.

As a child matures, the struggle to "cut the apron strings" ensues. The child demands independence. It is difficult for parents, who by neces-

Richard (left) and Chris (right), father and son, in the documentary *Pop and Me* (1999). Photograph © Erik Arnesen.

sity have been in control for so long to relinquish that control. The child is always "my baby"—but at a certain point the child cannot accept that label. The love becomes strained—but seldom snaps. *Pop and Me* captures the love between parent and child, the controlling nature of the parent, and the demand for independence on the part of the child.

The film presents interviews with fathers from around the world. Though there are variations on the manner in which love is expressed, an amazing similarity between responses becomes apparent. Of course, there are examples of fathers who do not fulfill their parental duties; the children of such fathers invariably express the immense void they feel every day.

If you view the other documentaries listed in this book, you will never forget Tammy Faye from *The Eyes of Tammy Faye* or Fred Leuchter from *Mr. Death*. Now you will be exposed to the unforgettable journey of Richard Roe and his son Chris. You won't forget them!

Watch the movie.

Questions to ponder:

1. Before the trip begins, Chris says, "As far as us getting along, I don't know — we'll see." On such a trip, what tensions might arise between parent and adult child that probably would not arise between two friends who travel together?

2. One of the sons interviewed says, "I had what a father is supposed to be.... If I wanted to draw a blueprint, I mean, I'd draw this man as my dad." What characteristics would you include in such a blueprint? Would you list the same characteristics for the ideal *mother*?

3. Many times during the film, a father or a child begins to shed tears. As a father, I also was moved to tears. Why does a child's expression of love for a parent, and vice versa, bring forth tears?

4. The bungee jump at the end of the film clearly brings Richard and Chris closer together. Why? Does that action indicate that parent and child should do daring things together?

ADDITIONAL RECOMMENDATIONS
FOR FILMS DEALING WITH LOVE

Casablanca (1942). One of the greatest films of all time. *Citizen Kane* is usually ranked as the greatest, as it is in the American Film Institute's list of the top 100 American movies. The AFI ranks *Casablanca* as number two. "Round up the usual suspects" is an unforgettable line. Humphrey Bogart, Ingrid Bergman, Claude Rains and Peter Lorre give performances that belong to the ages.

City Lights (1931). In 1931, talkies were taking over. Charlie Chaplin stayed with what he did best and made *City Lights*, another (almost) silent movie. The film offers two transcendent scenes. One is at the beginning of the film in which speeches are made at the unveiling of a statue. In that sequence, Chaplin pokes fun at talkies. The other scene is the last — it will break the hearts of all but the coldest viewer.

Pretty Woman (1990). Julia Robert's break-through role. Regularly compared to *Cinderella* — a lowly, but beautiful, girl finds her Prince Charming. Richard Gere is the Prince Charming in this film.

Harold and Maude (1971). In 1971, no one would think this film would be venerated all the way into the next century. Though not a Julia

Roberts/Richard Gere movie, it's a fairy tale romance, nonetheless. One of the American Film Institute's Top 100 Love Stories. Seventy-nine-year-old Maude and 20-year-old Harold! Unbelievable? Nope — believable! Watch the film.

Manhattan (1979). If you liked *Hannah and Her Sisters* (Movie 9), *Manhattan* is the next Woody Allen film to see. Woody will be Woody, and his supporting cast (Diane Keaton, Mariel Hemingway and Meryl Streep) provide great support. Great scene under the Brooklyn Bridge.

The Graduate (1967). You may think I'm crazy, but is the main reason Mrs. Robinson opposes Benjamin marrying her daughter Elaine the fact that it would be an incestuous union? (Are Elaine's father and Benjamin's father the same person?) Just a question. Dustin Hoffman and Katharine Ross backed up by Simon and Garfunkel — you couldn't ask for anything more.

Dirty Dancing (1987). What's dirty about it? Almost all dancing is sexual. So what? This film and *Ghost* are the best in Patrick Swayze's repertoire. Jennifer Grey never found another role to match the one in *Dirty Dancing*. Can you believe that three years before they made *Dirty Dancing*, Swayze and Grey were teamed up in the dud *Red Dawn*?

Gone with the Wind (1939). I've seen *Gone with the Wind* five times and I've fallen asleep every time. You gotta love it, though!

Moulin Rouge (2001). Love it or hate it — but if you hate it, you should try again to love it. Nicole Kidman regularly takes chances with challenging roles and regularly pulls them off. *Moulin Rouge* is no exception. A visually stunning movie.

Circle of Friends (1995). Irish soap opera. My daughter and I loved it when it was released in America. The Irish premiere came later, and as we were touring Ireland, we saw the movie again in Dublin. We visited various sites where scenes were filmed. (Tracking down actual film locations is a *real* adventure. On a recent trip to New Zealand, my daughter and I visited *Lord of the Rings* sites.)

Much Ado About Nothing (1993). The Bard's work captured by Kenneth Branagh. Silly, but brilliant. The all-star cast is clearly having fun. Highlights: the sparring between Benedick (Branagh) and Beatrice (Emma Thompson) plus Michael Keaton hamming it up as Dogberry. Denzel Washington as Don Pedro is also a pleasure. Keanu Reeves is not quite believable as Don John, however.

Cyrano de Bergerac (1990). Gerard Depardieu as the lovable person connected to the schnoz. The film perfectly captures the humor, warmth
and tragedy of Edmond Rostand's play. See Depardieu also in *The
Return of Martin Guerre* (Movie 2).

An Affair to Remember (1957). Do not bother with the 1994 remake starring Warren Beatty and Annette Bening. Those two actors are poor
replacements for Cary Grant and Deborah Kerr. Love on an ocean
liner.

Love Story (1970). Eric Segal's novel was a huge bestseller. It's a melo-
dramatic film, but you will never have to say you're sorry you watched
it. *Love Story* could also be listed in Chapter 9 (Death).

American Love Story (1999). Over eight hours in length, this PBS documentary is about the love found in an interracial family. Why watch
the antics of the Osbournes or the shallow material of *The Real World*
when there are documentaries like this?

Eyes Wide Shut (1999). Warning: Sexually explicit material. Stanley
Kubrick died a few months before the release of this, his last masterpiece. Tom Cruise and Nicole Kidman explore the effects of
infidelity.

Punch Drunk Love (2002). If *Man on the Moon* (1999), *The Truman Show*
(Movie 23), and *Eternal Sunshine of the Spotless Mind* (2004) provided Jim Carrey with opportunities to rise above lowbrow comedy,
Punch Drunk Love was Adam Sandler's chance. (In his next movie
he backslid into the lowly *Anger Management*.) Sandler does not possess great range, but his style is perfect for the character of Barry
Egan, a klutz who looks for a meaningful relationship but doesn't
know how to find one — or what to do when one becomes available.
Finally, he finds Lena (Emily Watson).

Cold Mountain (2003). Nicole Kidman wearing 21st century clothing
during the American Civil War. Jude Law going through hell to get
to Nicole.

17

Puzzlers

The three puzzlers in this chapter ("The Usual Suspects," "Memento," and "Mulholland Drive") contain brilliantly conceived plots. They are fun to watch even if you will never understand everything that is going on. If you work at it — if you don't just give up — you *will* understand a lot.

Movie 72: *The Usual Suspects*

Director: Bryan Singer; 2 hours, 2 minutes; 1995
Watch the movie.

Questions to ponder:

1. By the end of the movie, no matter how confused you might be, you should at least realize that Verbal Kint (Kevin Spacey) is Keyser Soze. Why does Keyser Soze kill the Hungarian who was cowering in the boat? Why does he kill Keaton (Gabriel Byrne)? While grilling Verbal, Dave Kujan (Chazz Palminteri) announces that Keaton's girlfriend Edie has been killed. At the time he announces that news, Dave thinks Keaton was Keyser Soze. Of course, he is wrong. Verbal had Edie killed. Why?

2. Again, before realizing that he had been duped, Dave thinks Keaton is Keyser Soze. Does Verbal lead Dave to this interpretation or does Dave come up with it by himself?

3. What evidence is there that Verbal is indeed Keyser Soze? Is there a Keyser Soze who really killed his wife and children in order to get to their attackers?

4. You may have missed it, but the hat and coat that Keyser Soze wears is shown hanging on the wall next to the terrorized Hungarian who is subsequently killed by Keyser Soze. When Dave argues that Keaton is Keyser Soze, there is a quick shot of Keaton wearing the hat and coat.

From left to right: Kevin Pollak, Stephen Baldwin, Benicio Del Toro, Gabriel Byrne and Kevin Spacey are *The Usual Suspects* (1995).

When Dave finally realizes that Verbal is the guilty one, Verbal is seen wearing the hat and coat. (That shot is followed by an even quicker sequence showing each of the other "usual suspects" — Keaton, McManus (Stephen Baldwin), Fenster (Benicio Del Toro) and Hockney (Kevin Pollack) — dead. They were all victims of Keyser Soze. Why would Verbal put on that hat and coat?

5. Clearly, a great deal of Verbal's testimony to Dave is false. For example, there was no Redfoot. Verbal borrowed the name "Redfoot" from the alias of a black woman who is highlighted on a wanted poster on the bulletin board. What other parts of Verbal's testimony are false?

6. Did Verbal, perhaps with the help of his front man "Kobayashe" (Pete Postlethwaite), set up the original lineup in order to get these particular "usual suspects" together? That way, Verbal could arrange that they would all be together in order to maneuver them to attack the boat. But if that is the case, why wouldn't he have had Kobayashe merely contact them separately and enlist their help? (Note: the name "Kobayashe" is not the real name of the front man. Verbal borrowed that name from

the name "Kobayashe Porcelain" imprinted on the coffee cup held by Dave during his interrogation.)

7. After watching the movie, you know Verbal is Keyser Soze. Look at the opening sequence of the movie again. The voice of Keyser Soze is heard before Keaton is shot. If it was clearly Kevin Spacey's voice, the viewer might guess that Verbal was Keyser Soze. The problem is, it is not clearly Spacey's voice. Is that a weakness in the movie? Can you spot any other apparent weaknesses?

Movie 73: *Memento*

Director: Christopher Nolan; 1 hour, 53 minutes; 2000

Warning: This film contains violence and foul language, and endangers the viewer's brain cells by making the brain think in a manner contrary to its natural tendency to project into the future and see things chronologically.

Watch the movie.

Guy Pearce as Leonard in *Memento* (2000).

Questions to ponder:

1. Who is Leonard (Guy Pearce) talking to on the telephone in the black and white scenes?

2. Is there really a Sammy Jenkis (Stephen Tobolowsky)? Was Leonard projecting his own condition onto a fictional person? Leonard says that Sammy is a patient in a mental hospital. Is it really Leonard who is the mental patient? (For an instant, there is a glimpse of Leonard as a patient in the mental ward. Watch carefully the scene in which Sammy sits peacefully in the asylum!) Is Leonard an escapee from a mental hospital who goes on a hunt for his wife's "killer"? Did Leonard kill his wife by giving her too much insulin? (There is a quick scene showing Leonard giving his wife an insulin shot! However, Leonard denies that his wife had diabetes, and that should have been a real memory.)

3. There is a scene in which Leonard is lying in bed with his wife. On his chest is a tattoo that contains the words "I've done it." *That* cannot be a memory. Are there other memories Leonard believes are real, but aren't?

4. Does Teddy (Joe Pantoliano) maneuver Leonard to kill Jimmy? Why?

5. Teddy shows a photograph that he says is of a happy Leonard after having just killed his wife's assailant. Was that murder orchestrated by Teddy? Could there have been other murders?

6. At the end of the film there comes a scene that is chronologically the *first* in the colored sequence. In that scene, why does Leonard destroy the picture of himself looking jubilant after supposedly killing his wife's attacker? He then stops at a tattoo parlor to have Teddy's license-plate number tattooed on his body. Interpret what is going on here.

7. Natalie (Carrie-Anne Moss) has Leonard track down Dodd, hoping Leonard will kill him. (Dodd is the one Leonard fights and puts in a closet.) Why does Natalie want Leonard to kill Dodd?

8. Why did Leonard put on Jimmy's clothes? (He also takes Jimmy's car after killing him.)

Movie 74: *Mulholland Drive*

Director: David Lynch; 2 hours, 27 minutes; 2001

Directions: Don't let *Mulholland Drive* discourage you. Try to enjoy this David Lynch masterpiece. Appreciate the fine acting of Naomi Watts

Naomi Watts (left) and Laura Elena Harring (right) in David Lynch's *Mul-holland Drive* (2001).

and Laura Elena Harring. After watching the film, try to determine what the heck happened to its characters. After you've made an authentic attempt to interpret the movie, turn to the "Questions to Ponder."

Watch the movie.

My interpretation of what happens in the movie:

Diane and Betty (Naomi Watts) are the same person. Camilla and Rita (Laura Elena Harring) are the same. After winning a jitterbug contest, Diane wants to become a movie star. Her aunt dies and leaves her money, which makes it possible for Diane to move to Hollywood and attempt to "make it." She falls in love with Camilla. Camilla, however, wins a part in a movie directed by Adam (Justin Theroux). Diane wanted that part. In addition, Camilla gets Adam, who announces at the party that he and Camilla are to be married. Diane starts to fall apart and ends up arranging to have a hit man kill Camilla. Diane enters the fantasy world of Betty, a name borrowed from the waitress in the restaurant. That fantasy world is shown during the first two-thirds of the movie. The scene in the theater where Betty becomes aware that a tape is being played and that reality is not as it seems is the scene in which she realizes she has been living in a fantasy world. Diane kills herself as demons (the elderly couple and the homeless man seen behind the diner) possess her.

Questions to ponder:

1. What is the meaning of the blue box and the blue key that opens it? Is there any connection between that blue key and the blue key that will indicate Camilla has been killed?

2. The elderly couple seen at the beginning of the movie with Diane as she arrives in L.A. becomes the demons who taunt Diane at the end. Who are they?

3. Why does the homeless man appear as a monster? The homeless man also has the blue box in one scene. Why?

4. Coco (Ann Miller), the manager of the apartment, appears at the party off Mulholland Drive. Who is she?

5. The cowboy (Monty Montgomery) can also be seen passing by at the party. Who is he and what role does he play in Diane's fantasy?

6. Rita finds a great deal of money in her purse. Is that the same money Diane gives to the hit man? What is going on here?

If you enjoyed *Mulholland Drive*, also try Lynch's *Lost Highway* (1997) and *Blue Velvet* (1986).

AN ADDITIONAL PUZZLER

Adaptation (2002). *Adaptation*'s screenwriter is the brilliant Charlie Kaufman, who also gave us *Being John Malkovich* (1999). Kaufman regularly startles the viewer with stunning plot shifts. The first time I viewed *Adaptation*, I felt the second half was a letdown. It isn't a letdown—I just didn't understand what was going on. In the film, Nicolas Cage plays Charlie Kaufman *and* Charlie's real or imagined twin brother, Donald. Cage is so much better in challenging roles like these than in junky action movies like *The Rock* and *Con Air*. Meryl Streep is not as convincing in the role of Susan Orlean, the author of a non-fiction book entitled *The Orchid Thief*, nor is Chris Cooper as John Larouche, who is the stealer of orchids. In the movie, Orlean is attracted to Larouche, and *that* I simply could not buy.

18

The Love of Movies

Movie 75: *Cinema Paradiso — The New Version*

Director: Guiseppe Tornatore; 2 hours, 53 minutes; 1989

I decided to end this book with a movie that will warm your heart. Also, since you must love movies (or you wouldn't be perusing this book), you'll appreciate the main theme of *Cinema Paradiso*. You'll never forget a small boy named Salvatore (Salvatore Cascio) and his friend Alfredo (Philippe Noiret), the projectionist at Cinema Paradiso.

And, perhaps, you'll hope I am working on a sequel to this book. Thanks for visiting.

Watch the movie.

Questions to ponder:

1. Why doesn't Alfredo tell the teenage Salvatore (Marco Leonardi) that Elena (Agnese Nano) had come to the Cinema Paradiso to give information on how Salvatore could contact her? Was Alfredo right to keep that knowledge from Salvatore?

2. Why doesn't Salvatore return to his hometown until after Alfredo's death? Why doesn't Alfredo want Salvatore to return?

3. What is the meaning of Alfredo's last gift to Salvatore — the film clips of people kissing?

4. Was the older Salvatore (Jacques Perrin) right to end the affair with the older Elena (Brigette Fossey)?

Philippe Noiret (left) and Salvatore Cascio in *Cinema Paradiso* (1989).

189

Notes

Chapter 1

1. *Enquiries Concerning Human Understanding and Concerning the Principles of Morals*, Oxford University Press: Oxford, 1975, p. 19.
2. *Op. cit.* p. 18.
3. *Op. cit.* p. 17.
4. *Op. cit.* p. 25.
5. *Ibid.*
6. *Op. cit.* p. 26.
7. Natalie Zemon Davis, *The Return of Martin Guerre* (Cambridge: Harvard University Press, 1983).
8. Davis, p. 88.
9. Davis, p. 90.
10. *New York Times*, 4 November 2001.
11. From an excerpt of his book *On Directing Film* in *Roger Ebert's Book of Film* (New York: W.W. Norton, 1997), p. 670.
12. Quote from Akira Kurosawa in *Roger Ebert's Book of Film*, (New York: W.W. Norton, 1997) pp. 484–485.

Chapter 2

1. John Stuart Mill, *Utilitarianism* (Indianapolis: Bobbs-Merrill, 1957), p. 10.
2. Jeremy Bentham, *The Principles of Morals and Legislation* (New York: Prometheus Books, 1988), p. 30.
3. *Ibid.*
4. Mill, p. 11.
5. *Op. cit.* p. 13.
6. *Op. cit.* p. 14.
7. *Op. cit.* p. 12

Chapter 3

1. Immanuel Kant, *Foundation of the Metaphysics of Morals*, trans. Lewis White Beck (Indianapolis: Bobbs-Merril, 1969), p. 20.
2. Kant, p. 44.
3. Kant, pp. 45–46.
4. Kant, pp. 46–47.

Chapter 4

1. Heidegger is usually listed with the atheistic existentialists; however, I strongly disagree with that classification.
2. *My Dinner with Andre,* Wallace Shawn and Andre Gregory (New York: Grove Press, 1981), p. 20.
3. Friedrich Nietzsche, *Thus Spoke Zarathustra*, trans. by Walter Kaufmann (New York: Viking, 1966), pp. 17–19.

Chapter 5

1. Quoted in Samuel Stumph, *Elements of Philosophy* (3rd Edition) (New York: McGraw-Hill, 1993), p. 492.

Chapter 6

1. Check and for two interesting papers from *The Journal of Religion and Film*. The papers are "Bess, the Christ Figure?: Theological Interpretations of 'Breaking the Waves'" by Linda Mercadante, and "Transgressing Goodness in 'Breaking the Waves'" by Irena S.M. Makarushka. *The*

Journal of Religion and Film is a good source for readable papers on religious issues in film such as *The Decalogue, The Rapture* and *The Apostle*.

2. Roger Ebert, *The Great Movies* (New York: Broadway Books, 2002), pp. 128, 130.

3. Michael Wilmington, *The A List: The National Society of Film Critics 100 Essential Films*, edited by Jay Carr (Cambridge MA: De Capo, 2002), p. 83.

4. Ebert, p. 130.

5. Martin Buber, *I and Thou*, translated by Walter Kaufmann (New York: Simon and Schuster, 1970).

Chapter 7

1. Plato, *Plato: The Collected Dialogues*, edited by Edith Hamilton and Huntington Cairns (New York: Pantheon Books, 1961), pp. 747–750.

2. Albert Camus, *The Myth of Sisyphus* (Knopf: New York, 1955), p. 91.

3. Rene Descartes, *The Philosophical Works of Descartes*, Volume I, translated by Elizabeth S. Haldane and G.R.T. Ross (London: Cambridge University Press, 1972), pp. 145–146.

4. William F. Lawhead, *The Philosophical Journey*, 2nd edition (Boston: McGraw-Hill, 2003), p. 456. Lawhead gives credit to Robert Nozick, *Anarchy, State and Utopia* (New York: Basic Books, 1974), pp. 42–43.

Chapter 8

1. Henry David Thoreau, *Civil Disobedience and Other Essays* (Doner Publications: New York, 1997), p. 7.

2. Thoreau, p. 8.

3. Thoreau, pp. 19–30.

4. Thoreau, p. 39.

Chapter 9

1. Martin Heidegger, *Being and Time*, translated by John Macquarrie and Ed-

ward Robinson (New York: Harper and Row, 1962), p. 294.

2. *Op. cit.* p. 235.

3. David Hume, *Enquiries Concerning Human Understanding and Concerning the Principles of Morals* (Oxford: Oxford University Press, 1975), p. 110.

Chapter 10

1. Bosley Crowther in *The New York Times Guide to the Best 1,000 Movies Ever Made*, edited by Peter M. Nichols (New York: New York Times Book, 1999), p. 645.

Chapter 11

1. This idea, that most viewers in 1915 probably did not zero in on the irrational social stereotyping while watching the film, is expressed in an excellent two-part evaluation of *The Birth of a Nation* by Roger Ebert. The two parts appeared in the Chicago *Sun Times* on March 30, 2003, and April 13, 2003.

2. William H. Chafe, "Mississippi Burning" in *Past Imperfect: History According to the Movies*, edited by Mark C. Carnes (New York: Henry Holt, 1995), p. 277. This book provides excellent analyses of such movies as *Spartacus, Mutiny on the Bounty, Bonnie and Clyde, Gandhi* and *JFK*. Watching the movies which are covered in the Carnes book and then reading the articles is a real intellectual adventure that provides hours of rewarding viewing.

3. Vincent Canby in *The New York Times Guide to the Best 1,000 Movies Ever Made*, edited by Peter M. Nichols (New York: New York Times Books, 1999), p. 230.

4. Jay Carr, editor, *The A list: The National Society of Film Critics' 100 Essential Films* (Cambridge MA: DaCapo Press, 2002), p. 9.

5. Roger Ebert, *The Great Movies* (New York: Broadway Books, 2002), p. 142.

Chapter 13

1. Simone de Beauvoir, *The Second Sex* (New York: Random House, 1951), p. 305.
2. *Ibid.*, p. 315.
3. *Ibid.*, pp. 345-346.
4. *Ibid.*, p. 376.
5. *Ibid.*, p. 400.
6. *Ibid.*, p. 495.
7. *Ibid.*, p. 573.
8. *Ibid.*, p. 574.
9. *Ibid.*, p. 649.
10. Friedrich Nietzsche, *Thus Spoke Zarathustra*, translated by Walter Kaufmann (New York: Viking Press), pp. 71-74.
11. Marie-Henri-Beyle Stendhal, *On Love* (Cambridge, MA: DaCapo Press, 1988).

Chapter 14

1. Jeremy Bentham, "An Essay on Paederasty" in *Philosophy and Sex,* 3rd Edition, by Robert B. Baker, Kathleen J. Wininger and Frederick A. Elliston (Prometheus Books: Amherst, N.Y., 1998), p. 351.

Chapter 16

1. Aristotle, *The Basic Works of Aristotle*, ed. by Richard McKean (New York: Random House, 1941), p. 1061.
2. Martin Buber, *I and Thou*, translated by Ronald Gregor Smith (New York: Scribner's, 1958), p. 11.
3. *Op. cit.* p. 34.
4. *Op. cit.* p. 6.
5. *Op. cit.* p. 128.

Bibliography

Aristotle. *The Basic Works of Aristotle*, ed. by Richard McKean. New York: Random House, 1941.

Armstrong, John. *Conditions of Love: The Philosophy of Intimacy*. New York: W.W. Norton, 2003.

Babitt, Susan E., and Sue Campbell, eds. *Racism and Philosophy*. Ithaca, NY: Cornell University Press, 1999.

Badhwar, Neera Kapur, ed. *Friendship: A Philosophical Reader*. Ithaca, NY: Cornell University Press, 1993.

Bawer, Bruce. *A Place at the Table: The Gay Individual in American Society*. New York: Simon and Schuster, 1994.

Beauchamp, Tom L., and Robert M. Veatch. *Ethical Issues in Death and Dying*. 2nd ed. Upper Saddle River, NJ: Prentice-Hall, 1996.

Bedau, Hugo Adam. *Civil Disobedience in Focus*. New York: Routledge, 1991.

Bentham, Jeremy. "An Essay on Paederasty" in *Philosophy and Sex*, 3rd ed., Robert Baker, Frederich Elliston, and Kathleen J. Wininger, eds. New York: Prometheus, 1998.

_____. *The Principles of Morals and Legislation*. New York: Prometheus Books, 1988.

Buber, Martin. *I and Thou*. Translated by Ronald Gregor Smith. New York: Scribner's, 1958.

Camus, Albert. *The Myth of Sisyphus*. Translated by Justin O'Brien. New York: Knopf, 1955. See the title essay on pages 119–123.

_____. *The Stranger*. New York: Random House, 1988.

Canby, Vincent, Janet Maslin, and the Film Critics of the *New York Times. The New York Times Guide to the Best 1,000 Movies Ever Made*, Peter M. Nichols, ed. New York: Random House, 1999.

Carnes, Mark C. *Past Imperfect: History According to the Movies*. New York: Henry Holt, 1995.

Carr, Jay, ed. *The A List: The National Society of Film Critics' 100 Essential Films*. New York: DaCapo, 2002.

Cohen, Marshall, Thomas Nagle, and Thomas Scanlon, eds. *War and Moral Responsibility*. Princeton: Princeton University Press, 1974.

Cook, David A. *A History of Narrative Film*. 3rd ed. New York: W.W. Norton, 1996.

Cornell, Drucilla, ed. *Feminism and Pornography*. Oxford: Oxford University Press, 2000.

Davis, Natalie Zemon. *The Return of Martin Guerre*. Cambridge, MA: Harvard University Press, 1983.

DeBeauvoir, Simone. *The Second Sex*. New York: Vintage, 1989.

DeRose, Keith, and Ted A. Warfield. *Skepticism: A Contemporary Reader*. Oxford: Oxford University Press, 1999.

DeSpelder, Lynne Ann and Albert Lee Strickland. *The Last Dance: Encountering Death and Dying*. 6th ed. New York, McGraw-Hill, 2001.

Dines, Gail, Robert Jensen and Ann Russo. *Pornography: The Production and Consumption of Inequality*. New York: Routledge, 1997.

Ebert, Roger. *The Great Movies*. New York: Broadway, 2002.

_____. *Robert Ebert's Book of Film*. New York: W.W. Norton, 1996.

Gandhi, Mahatma. *The Essential Gandhi: An Anthology of His Writings on His Life, Work and Ideas*, ed. by Louis Fischer. New York: Vintage, 2002.

Gilbert, Martin. *The Holocaust: A History of the Jews of Europe During the Second World War*. New York: Holt Rinehart and Winston, 1986.

Goldberg, David Theo. *Anatomy of Racism*. Minneapolis: University of Minnesota Press, 1990.

Harvey, Philip D., and Nadine Strossen. *The Government vs. Erotica: The Siege of Adam and Eve*. New York: Prometheus, 2001.

Heidegger, Martin. *Being and Time*. Translated by John Macquarrie and Edward Robinson. New York: Harper and Row, 1962.

Hilberg, Paul. *The Destruction of the European Jews*. 3rd ed. New Haven, CT: Yale University Press, 2003.

Honderich, Ted. *How Free Are You? The Determinism Problem*. Oxford: Oxford University Press, 1993.

Hume, David. *Enquiries Concerning Human Understanding and Concerning the Principles of Morals*. 3rd ed. Oxford: Oxford University Press, 1985.

_____. *A Treatise of Human Nature*. 2nd ed. Oxford: Oxford University Press, 1978.

Kael, Pauline. *I Lost It at the Movies: Film Writings 1954–1965*. London: Marion Boyars Publishers, 1994.

Kant, Immanuel. *Critique of Practical Reason*. 3rd ed. Translated by Lewis White Beck. New York: Macmillan, 1993.

_____. *Foundations of the Metaphysics of Morals*. Translated by Lewis White Beck. Indianapolis: Bobbs-Merrill, 1969.

Kaufmann, Walter, ed. *Existentialism From Dostoevsky to Sartre*. New York: Meridian, 1975.

Kierkegaard, Soren. *Fear and Trembling/Repetition*. Princeton: Princeton University Press, 1983.

Lewis, C.S. *A Grief Observed*. San Francisco: Harper, 2001.

_____. *The Problem of Pain*. New York: Simon and Schuster, 1996.

Litch, Mary M. *Philosophy Through Film*. New York: Routledge, 2002.

Loftus, David. *Watching Sex: How Men Really Respond to Pornography*. New York: Thunder's Mouth Press, 2002.

Mates, Benson. *The Skeptic Way: Sextus Empiricus's Outlines of Pyrrhonism*. Oxford: Oxford University Press, 1996.

Mill, John Stuart. *The Subjection of Women*. Cambridge, MA: Hackett, 1989.

_____. *Utilitarianism*. Indianapolis: Bobbs-Merrill, 1957.

Nietzsche, Friedrich. *Thus Spoke Zarathustra*. Translated by Walter Kaufmann. New York: Viking, 1966.

Norton, David L., and Mary F. Kille, eds. *Philosophies of Love*. Totowa, NJ: Rowan and Littlefield, 1988.

Pelikan, Jaroslav. *The World Treasury of Modern Religious Thought*. Boston: Little, Brown and Company, 1990.

Pereboom, Derk. *Living Without Free Will*. Cambridge: Cambridge University Press, 2001.

Plato. *Plato: The Collected Dialogues*. Edith Hamilton and Huntington Cairns, eds. New York: Pantheon Books, 1961.

Porter, Burton F. *Philosophy Through Fiction and Film*. Upper Saddle River, NJ: Prentice Hall, 2004.

Sartre, Jean-Paul. *Nausea*. Translated by Lloyd Alexander. New York: New Direction, 1964.

_____. *No Exit and Three Other Plays*. New York: Random House, 1949.

Shawn, Wallace, and Andre Gregory. *My Dinner with Andre*. New York: Grove Press, 1981.

Smith, Huston. *The World's Religions: Our Great Wisdom Traditions*. San Francisco: Harper, 1991.

Soble, Alan. *Pornography, Sex and Feminism*. New York: Prometheus, 2002.

Solomon, Robert C., *About Love*. Lanham, MD: Madison Books, 2001.

_____, ed. *Existentialism*. New York: Random House, 1974.

Strossen, Nadine. *Defending Pornography*. New York: Anchor, 1996.

Sullivan, Andrew. *Virtually Normal*. New York: Vintage, 1996.

Swinburne, Richard, ed. *Miracles*. New York: Macmillan, 1989.

Thomas, Laurence, and Michael Levin. *Sexual Orientation and Human Rights*. Lanham, MD: Rowan and Littlefield, 1999.

Thompson, Kristen, and David Bordwell. *Film History*. 2nd ed. Boston: McGraw Hill, 2003.

Thoreau, Henry David. *Civil Disobedience and Other Essays*. New York: Dover, 1997.

Wasserstrom, Richard A., ed. *War and Morality*. Belmont, CA: Wadsworth, 1970.

Williams, Clifford, ed. *On Love and Friendship*. Boston: Jones and Bartlett, 1995.

Wollstonecraft, Mary. *A Vindication of the Rights of Women*. New York: Dover, 1996.

Index

Abandon Ship 23–25
About Schmidt 33, 38–40, 140
Abraham 52, 57
absurd hero 37
absurdity of existence 33, 41
Adams, Joey Lauren 154
Adaptation 188
The Adventures of Priscilla, Queen of the Desert 160
An Affair to Remember 182
Affleck, Ben 66, 153–154
agape 167, 176
Agnes of God 66
Aiello, Danny 120–121
Akira Kurosawa's Dreams 17
Akkad, Moustapha 51
All Quiet on the Western Front 114
All That Heaven Allows 123
Allegory of the Cave 67–69, 81
Allen, Woody 33–35, 41, 101, 181
American History X 119–120
American Love Story 182
analytic/synthetic distinction 5–7
Anderson, Adisa 150
Anderson, Jane 155
Anger Management 182
Annaud, Jean-Jacques 171
Annie Hall 35
anxiety (angst) 32–42
Apocalypse Now Redux 113
Apostle 55–56
Arenas, Reynaldo 159
Aristotle 168
Armstrong, Karen 52
Arquette, David 133
Artemisia 134, 145–147
Artemisia Gentileschi 146
Atchison, Doug 164–165
Attenborough, Richard 84, 87

Audran, Stephane 177–178
Augustine 68
Autumn Spring 102
Avery, Margaret 79
Axel, Gabriel 176
Ayres, Lew 114

Babette's Feast 60, 167, 176–178
Badham, John 92
Baka, Misoslaw 62
Baker, Dylan 122
Bakker, Jim 58–59
Bakker, Tammy 58–59, 179
Baldwin, Stephen 184
Balk, Fairuza 151
Bananas 35
Bancroft, Anne 66
Bankhead, Tallulah 25
Baradem, Javier 159
Baranowski, Henryk 60
Barbato, Randy 58
Barbie, Klaus 132–133
Barbusse, Henri 108
Barcis, Artur 64
Bardini, Aleksander 61
Barelkowska, Maja 63
Barley, Fenton 58
Barrabas 66
Barry Lyndon 111
Barton Fink 18
Batman 74
Baye, Nathalie 10, 13
Baynaud, Erwan 170
Bazen, Andre 12
Beatty, Warren 182
Bedrooms and Hallways 160
Before Night Falls 159
Being and Time 90
Being John Malkovich 188

Bell, Jamie 69–70
Ben Hur 65
Bendix, William 25
Benigni, Roberto 126, 131–132
Bening, Annette 182
Benthem, Jeremy 19–20, 153
Berenger, Tom 25, 113
Bergen, Candice 85
Bergman, Ingmar 99–101
Bergman, Ingrid 180
Berkeley, Xander 84
Bertolucci, Bernardo 53
Biedrynska, Adrianna 61
billiard ball example 8
Billy Elliott 69–70, 144, 147
The Birth of a Nation 116
Bitorajac, Rene 112
Bjornstrand, Gunnar 99
Blaszczyk, Ewa
Blind Chance 47
Blue Velvet 188
Blues Brothers 75
Bocanegra, Elisa 72
Bogart, Humphrey 180
Bomba, Abraham 128
Bonnaire, Sandrine 169–170
Boogie Nights 164, 166
Boys Don't Cry 160
Branagh, Kenneth 181
Bread and Roses 86
Breaking the Waves 56–57, 68
The Bridge on the River Kwai 113–114
Bridges, Jeff 91
The Bridges of Madison County 167, 172
Broadway Danny Rose 35
Broderick, Matthew 114
Brodsky, Vlastimil 102
Brody, Adrien 86, 126, 129
Brooks, Avery 119
Brown, John 81–82
Brumberg, Joan Jacobs 134
Bryan, William Jennings 66
Buber, Martin 32, 60, 176–178
Buddha 53–55
Burns, Edward 108, 174–174
Burstyn, Ellen 97
Buscemi, Steve 133
Byrne, Gabriel 183–184

Cage, Nicolas 186
Cagin, Philip 118

Caine, Michael 166
Calderon, Paul 71
Camus, Albert 32–34, 41, 69
Canby, Vincent 120
Cantarini, Giorgio 132
capital punishment 62, 94–95
Cardoso, Patricia 144
Cariou, Len 39
Caro, Niki 147
Carrey, Jim 72–74
Cartlidge, Katrin 56
Casablanca 104, 180
Cascio, Salvatore 189
Cassavetes, John 92–93
Castle-Hughes, Keisha 147–148
The Categorical Imperative 27–29
causality 8
The Celluloid Closet 157
Cervera, Jorge, Jr. 144–145
Cervi, Valentina 145–146
Chaney, James 117–118
Chaplin, Charlie 132, 180
Charles, Ray 82
Chasing Amy 153–155, 161, 167
Cher 142
Chocolat 102
Choudhury, Sarita 125
Chukhraj, Pavel 170
Cinema Paradiso 189
Circle of Friends 181
Citizen Kane 180
City Lights 180
civil disobedience 81–86
The Clansmen 116
A Clockwork Orange 47, 111, 165–166
Cobb, Humphrey 106
Cobb, Lee J. 9–10
Coen Brothers 18
Cold Mountain 182
Coleman, Dabney 151
The Color Purple 78–80, 133
Con Air 188
Conrad, Joseph 113
Coolidge, Martha 155
Cooper, Chris 188
Cooper, Gary 29–30
Coras, Jean de 10
Crane, Stephen 105
Cremer, Bruno 89
Cries and Whispers 101
Crimes and Misdemeanors 35, 41

Crisp, Quentin 157–158
The Critique of Practical Reason 27
The Critique of Pure Reason 27
Crouse, Lindsay 14
Cruise, Tom 182
The Crying Game 18
Crystal, Billy 168–169
Cyrano de Bergerac 14, 182

DaFoe, Willem 48–50, 113, 118–119
Daldry, Stephen 69
Damon, Matt 66, 108
Dare Call It Treason 107
Darrow, Clarence 66
Dash, Julie 148
Daughters of the Dust 148–150
Davies, Jeremy 109
Davis, Geena 138
Davis, Hope 39
Davis, Natalie Zemon 10,12
Dawson, Rosario 174
Day, Cora Lee 149–150
Dead Man Walking 94–95, 167
Dean, James 158
Dean, Loren 84
death 33, 87–103
DeBeauvoir, Simone 32–33, 134–137
The Decalogue 47, 59–65, 95, 176
Deconstructing Harry 35
Dee, Sandra 124
The Deer Hunter 113
"A Defense of Abortion" 142
DeGeneris, Ellen 156
DeGood, Michael 164–165
Del Toro, Benicio 184
Demme, Jonathan 156
Deneuve, Catherine 170
DeNiro, Robert 113
Depardieu, Gerard 10, 11, 13, 14, 182
Depp, Johnny 159
Dersu Uzala 17
deSade, Marquise 166
Descartes, René 75
Determinism 42–47, 106
deVito, Danny 74
Dickinson, Emily 82
Dirty Dancing 181
Dixon, Thomas, Jr. 116
Djuric, Branko 112
Do the Right Thing 120–122
Dr. Strangelove, or: How I Learned to

Stop Worrying and Love the Bomb
111
Dr. Zhivago 113
Dogma 66
Double Lives, Second Chances 59–60
Douglas, Kirk 106–107
Douglas, Santiago 72
Dray, Philip 118
Dreyfuss, Richard 93–93
dualism 96
du Tilh, Arnauld 12
Duvall, Robert 55–56, 113

East-West 167–171
Eastwood, Clint 172–173
Ebert, Roger 59, 121–122
Eckhart, Aaron 137–138
Edelstein, David 12–13
Edwards, Stacy 138
egocentric predicament 5
Eilber, Janet 93
Einstein, Albert 82
Eisenstadt, Debra 151
Ekerot, Bengt 99–100
Emmerich, Noah 73
Enquiry Concerning Human Understanding 5
Epstein, Rob 157
Ermey, Lee 110
Esposito, Giancarlo 121
ethical relativism 115
euthanasia 92–94
Everyone Says I Love You 35
Everything You Always Wanted to Know About Sex 35
existential rebellion 33
Existentialism 32–42, 90, 99, 139
The Exorcist 66
The Eyes of Tammy Faye 58–59, 162, 179
Eyes Wide Shut 111, 182

Falconetti, Renee 65
Faludi, Susan 134
Falwell, Jerry 162
Fanny and Alexander 101
Far from Heaven 123
Fargo 18
Farrow, Mia 34
fate 42–47, 106
Fearless 33, 90–92
Ferrera, America 144–145

The Field 25–26, 87, 167
Field, Sally 86
Firth, Peter 46
Fishburne, Laurence 75
Five East Pieces 41
flukes 44, 46, 62
Flynt, Larry 162–163
Fonda, Bridget 53
Fonda, Henry 9–10
Fonda, Jane 66, 151
Ford, John 114
Forman, Milos 162
Fossey, Bridgette 189
Foster, Jodie 12–13
Foundations of the Metaphysics of Morals 27
4 Little Girls 125
Frankenstein 160
Fraser, Brandon 160
Freeman, Morgan 114
Freidan, Betty 134
Frida 159
Friedman, Jeffrey 157
friendship 167–169
Full Metal Jacket 18, 104, 109–111
Furlong, Edward 120

Gajos, Janusz 61
Gandhi 68, 82, 84–85, 125
Garrard, Mary D. 146
Gattaca 82
Gavin, John 124
gay rights 152–160
Gere, Richard 12–13, 180–181
Ghost 102
Gibson, Mel 50
Gilbert, Martin 126
Girlfight 70–72
Glanzelius, Anton 102
Globisz, Krzysztof 62
Gloomy Sunday 133
Glory 114
Glover, Danny 78
Goddard, Paul 75
Gods and Monsters 160
Goldberg, Whoopi 78–79, 102, 115, 122
Goldstein, Steven 16
Gone with the Wind 181
Good Morning, Vietnam 114
Goodman, Andrew 117–118

The Gospel According to Saint Matthew 66
The Graduate 181
Graham, Heather 173
Grand Illusion 114
Grant, Cary 182
Grant, Earl 125
Grassler, Dr. Franz 128
The Great Dictator 132
The Great Escape 114
greatest happiness principle 19–26
Gregory, Andre 36–38
Grey, Jennifer 181
The Grey Zone 133
A Grief Observed 87
Griffith, D.W. 116–117
Guess Who's Coming to Dinner? 125
Guinness, Alec 113

Hackman, Gene 118
Hallstrom, Lasse 102
Hanks, Tom 108, 156–157
Hannah, James 46–47
Hannah and Her Sisters 33–35, 101, 167, 181
happiness machine 77–78
hard determinists 42
Hardy, Thomas 45–46
Harlan County, USA 35
Harold and Maude 180
Harrelson, Woody 162–163, 175
Harring, Laura Elena 187
Harris, Ed 72
Harris, Marjorie 165
Harris, Richard 25
Hawke, Ethan 83
Hawkins, Stephen 82
Hayden, Sterling 111
Haynes, Todd 123
Hayworth, Rita 82
Heart of Darkness 113
Hearts of Darkness — A Filmmaker's Apocalypse 113
Heche, Anne 143, 155
Hedwig and the Angry Inch 160
Heidegger, Martin 32, 35, 90
Hemingway, Mariel 181
Hepburn, Katharine 125
Hershey, Barbara 34, 48
Heston, Charlton 37, 53
High and Low 17

High Noon 29
Hilberg, Raul 128
Hitchcock, Alfred 25, 62–63
Hitler, Adolph 132–133
Hoffman, Dustin 181
Holbach, Baron d' 42–43
The Holocaust 33, 126–133
The Holocaust: A History of the Jews of Europe During the Second World War 126
Honglei, Sun 30
Hopkins, Anthony 87–88
The Horse Soldiers 114
Hotel Terminus: The Life and Times of Klaus Barbie 132–133
House of Games 14, 16, 133, 157
Howett, Peter 46
Hudson, Rock 123
Hume, David 5–9, 14, 98
Hurst, Fannie 123
Husbands and Wives 35
Huston, John 105

I and Thou 60, 176–178
If These Walls Could Talk, Part I 134, 142–143
If These Walls Could Talk, Part II 155–156
Ikiru 17
Imitation of Life 123–125
In the Bedroom 101
In the Company of Men 134, 137–138
The Incredible Hulk 74–75
Indecent Proposal 174–175
indeterminists 42
Indiana Jones and the Temple of Doom 1–2
Indochine 170
Inherit the Wind 65
Insdorf, Annette 59
insider/outsider distinction 54–55
Into the Arms of Strangers: Story of the Kindertransport 133
Into the Woods 72
Iris 159
Isaak, Chris 53
Islam 51–53, 66

Jackson, Desreta 79
Jackson, Mahalia 124
Janda, Krystyna 61

Jaspers, Karl 32
Jean de Florette/Manon of the Spring 14
Jesus 48–53, 57, 68
Jesus of Nazareth 66
Johnny Got His Gun 108, 114
Jones, Tommy Lee 74
Joyner-Kersee, Jackie 82
Jurassic Park 1

Kagemusha 17
Kant, Immanuel 6, 27–29, 109
Kaufman, Charlie 188
Kaye, Tony 119
Keaton, Diane 181
Keaton, Michael 181
Keitel, Harvey 48, 133
Kelly, Grace 29
Kennedy, John F. 82
Kerr, Deborah 182
Kidman, Nichole 181, 182
Kierkegaard, Soren 32–33
Kieslowski, Krzysztof 47, 59–65
King, Martin Luther, Jr. 67, 68, 85
Kingsley, Ben 84–85
Kinski, Nastassia 45–46
Kohler, Susan 124
Komorowska, Maja 60
Kopple, Barbara 35 ·
Koscialkowska, Maria 63
Kowalski, Wladyslaw 63
Kramer, Stanley 125
Kretschmann, Thomas 130
Kubrick, Stanley 106, 109–111, 182
Kulle, Jarl 178
Kurosawa, Akira 15–17
Kurosawa: A Documentary on the Acclaimed Director 17
Kusama, Karyn 70
Kyo, Machiko 15

Labute, Neal 137
Ladybird, Ladybird 134, 140–142
Lagerkvist, Par 66
Lahti, Christine 93
Lanzmann, Claude 115, 126, 128
The Last Days 129
The Last Temptation of Christ 48–50, 87
Latzko, Adolf Andreas 108
Law, Jude 83, 182
Lawrence, Jerome 65
Lawrence of Arabia 113

Lawson, Leigh 45–46
Lean, David 113
Lee, Canada 25
Lee, Robert E. 65
Lee, Spike 120–122, 125
Lenauer, Jean 37
Leonardi, Marco 189
Lethal Weapon II 2
Leuchter, Fred A. 130–131, 179
Leung, Tony 171
Levinson, Barry 114
Lewis, C.S. 87–89
Lewis, Gary 69
life after death 92, 96–99
A Life Apart: Hasidism in America 66
Life Is Beautiful 79, 126, 131–132
Lifeboat 25
The Limey 160
Lincoln, Abraham 82, 117
Linda, Boguslaw 63
Linklater, Richard 12
Little Buddha 53–55, 87
Loach, Ken 140
Lolita 111
Lonesome Dove 102
The Long Walk Home 115
The Lord of the Rings 109
Lorre, Peter 18, 180
Lost Highway 188
love 167–182
Love Story 182
The Lover 161, 171–172
Lubaszenko, Olaf 63
Lynch, David 186–188
Lynch, John 46
Lyne, Adrian 174

M 18
Machalica, Piotr 64
MacLaine, Shirley 102, 152
Macready, George 106
Macy, William H. 151
Madadayo 17
Malcolm X 112
Malle, Louis 35
Malloy Matt 137–138
Mamet, David 14, 151
Man on the Moon 182
Manhattan 35, 181
Manojlovic, Miki 146
Mantegna, Joseph 13

March, Jane 171
Marczewska, Teresa 63
Marsh, Fredric 65
Martins, Orlando 23
Matrix 74–78, 160
matters of fact 5–8, 10
Maudlin, Bill 105
McKellen, Ian 160
McKidd, Kevin 160
McMurtry, Larry 102
Meditations 75
Memento 160, 185–186
Men in War 108
Menshikov, Oleg 169
Merlet, Agnes 145
The Message 51–53
Metropolis 18
Meyer, Carl 65
Mifune, Toshiro 15, 17
Mighty Aphrodite 35
Mill, John Stuart 19–21, 71
Miller, Ann 188
Miller, Rebecca 150
Miller's Crossing 18
Mineo, Sal 158
Minority Report 84
Mississippi Burning 117
Mississippi Masala 125
Mr. Death 126, 130–131, 179
Mitchell, John Cameron 160
Modine, Matthew 110
Montgomery, Monty 188
Monty Python's The Life of Brian 66
Moore, Demi 102, 142–143, 175
Moore, Juanita 124
Moore, Julianne 123
Moore, Kaycee 149
moral relativists 21
Moretti, Nanni 101
Mori, Masayuki 17
Morissette, Alanis 66
Morris, Errol 130
Morris, Wayne 107
Moss, Carrie, Ann 75, 186
Moulin Rouge 181
Much Ado About Nothing 181
Muhammad 51–53
Muhammad: A Biography of the Prophet 52
Mulroney, Dermot 39
Murphy, Audie 105

My Dinner with Andre 33, 35–38, 104
My Life as a Dog 102
"The Myth of Sisyphus" 34
Nano, Agnese 189
Neeson, Liam 133
Network 68
Niccol, Andrew 82
Nicholson, Jack 38–39, 41, 74, 102
Nietzsche, Friedrich 32–33, 38, 67, 68
Night and Fog 133
Nine to Five 151
No Man's Land 104, 112–113
Noiret, Philippe 189
Nolan, Lloyd 23
Noland, Christopher 185
Norma Rae 86
Norton, Edward 119–120, 162
Not Without My Daughter 66
Nunn, Bill 121

Olbrychski, Daniel 61
Oleanna 151
Oliu, Ingrid 144
Once Were Warriors 147
One Flew Over the Cuckoo's Nest 41
Ontiveros, Lupe 144
Ophuls, Marcel 133
Ordinary People 102
other-worldly thought 32
Ozon, Francois 89

Paglia, Camille 134
Pakulnis, Maria 61
Palminteri, Chazz 183
Paltrow, Gwyneth 46–47
Pantoliano, Joe 77, 186
Paratene, Rawiri 147
Parker, Alan 117–119
Parton, Dolly 151
The Passion of Joan of Arc 65
The Passion of the Christ 50
Paths of Glory 104–108
Payne, Alexander 38
Pearce, Guy 160, 185–186
Pearce, Richard 122
Penn, Sean 94–95, 159
The People vs. Larry Flynt 162–163
Perez, Rosie 91
Perrin, Jacques 189
Persona 101
Personal Velocity 150

Petrie, Daniel 96
Pfeiffer, Michelle 74
Phaedo 96
Philadelphia 156–157
Philipchuck, Misha 171
Phoenix, Jaoquin 166
The Pianist 86, 126, 129–130
Piesiewicz, Krzystof 59
Pinkett-Smith, Jada 143
Plato 32, 67–70, 74–75, 81, 96
Platoon 113
Play It Again, Sam 35
Pleasantville 73
pleasure/pain calculus 19–20
Poitier, Sidney 125
Polanski, Roman 45, 126, 129
Pollak, Kevin 184
Pop and Me 167, 176, 178–180
The Pornographer 164–165
pornography 161–166
Posey, Parker 151
Power, Tyrone 23
predeterminists 42
Pretty Woman 180
Priest 66
Prolegomena to Any Future Metaphysics 27
Punch Drunk Love 182

Quaid, Dennis 123
Quills 166

racism 115–125
Radio Days 35
Raiders of the Lost Ark 1
Rains, Claude 180
Rambo 75
Rampling, Charlotte 89
Ran 17
The Rapture 66
Rashomon 15–17
Rawlins, Adrian 56
Rea, Stephen 18
Real Women Have Curves 144–145
Rear Window 62
reasonable doubt 9
The Rebel 33
Rebel Without a Cause 158
The Red Badge of Courage 104–106, 114
Red Beard 17
Redford, Robert 102, 175

Redgrave, Vanessa 155
Reeves, Keanu 53, 74–75, 181
Reiner, Rob 167
relations of ideas 5–6
Remarque, Erich Maria 108, 114
The Republic 67
Resurrection 96–99
The Return of Martin Guerre 10–14, 87, 182
Reynolds, Burt 164, 166
Rhapsody in August 17
The Road Home 29–31, 87
Robbins, Tim 94
Roberts, Julia 180–181
The Rock 188
Rock, Chris 66
Rock, Crissy 140–141
Rodriguez, Michelle 71
Roe, Chris 178–179
Roe, Richard 179
Rogers, Alva 150
Ross, Katherine 181
Rossellini, Isabella 91
Rostand, Edmond 182
Ruchti, Ulrich 111
Run, Lola, Run 47
Rush, Geoffrey 166
Rusmussen, Randy 111
Ryan, Meg 168–169

Sale, Richard 23
Sandler, Adam 182
Sarandon, Susan 95, 138–139
Sartre, Jean-Paul 32, 42
Saving Private Ryan 104, 108–109, 167
Savoca, Nancy 142
Schindler's List 79, 129, 133
Schultz, Dwight 122
Schwerner, Mickey 117–118
Scorcese, Martin 48
Scott, George C. 111
Scott, Ridley 138
The Second Sex 33, 134–137
Sedgwick, Kyra 151
Segal, Eric 182
Seldes, Marian 155
Sellers, Peter 111
Serrault, Michel 146
Seth, Roshan 125
The Seven Samurai 17
The Seventh Seal 99, 102

Sevigny, Chloe 156
sexism 134–151
Shadowlands 87–89, 102, 172
Shaw, Robert Gould 114
Shawn, Wallace 36–38
Shephard, Sam 98
Sheridan, Jim 25
Shimura, Takashi 17
Shine 166
The Shining 111
Shoah 115, 126–129
Show Me Love 159
Sidewalks of New York 173–174
Silence of the Lambs 18
A Simple Plan 18
Singer, Bryan 183
Sirk, Douglas 123–124
Skarsgard, Stellon 56–67
Skepticism 5–8
Sleeper 35
Sliding Doors 45–47, 167
Sling Blade 56
Smith, Huston 52
Smith, Kevin 153
Smoke Signals 147
Socrates 68, 96
soft determinists 42–43
Something About Mary 2
Sommersby 12–13
Sondheim, Stephen 72
The Son's Room 101
Sophie's Choice 133
Sorvino, Mia 133
Sovogovic, Filip 112
Spacek, Sissy 122, 143
Spacey, Kevin 183–184
Spartacus 111
Speilberg, Steven 78, 108, 133
Squibb, June 39
Srebnik, Simon 127
Stalag 17, 114
Stamp, Terence 160
Stanley Kubrick, Director: A Visual Analysis 111
Stanley Kubrick: 7 Films Analyzed 111
Steinem, Gloria 134
Stendahl 140
Stern, Stewart 158
Steward, James 62
Stone, Sharon 156
The Stranger 34, 41

Streep, Meryl 133, 172–173, 181, 188
Stuhr, Jerzy 65
Sun, Honglei 30
Swank, Hilary 160
Swayze, Patrick 102, 181
Sweet and Lowdown 35
The Sweet Hereafter 101
Szapolowska, Grazyna 63
Szpilman, Wladyslaw 126–130

Take the Money and Run 35
Tanovic, Danis 112
Taylor, Robert 75
Taylor, Sybil 111
The Ten Commandments 52
Terms of Endearment 102
Tesarz, Jan 62
Tess 45–46, 167
Tess of the d'Urbervilles 45
Thelma and Louise 138–140
Theroux, Justin 187
They Came to Cordura 113
The Thief 170
Thompson, Emma 181
Thomson, Judith Jarvis 142
Thoreau, Henry David 81–82
Thornton, Billy Bob 56
Throne of Blood 17
Thurman, Uma 83
Thus Spoke Zarathustra 67
Tillich, Paul 32
Tilly, Meg 66
Tirelli, Jaime 71
Tobolowsky, Stephen 186
Tomlin, Lily 151
Tornatore, Guiseppe 189
Torry, Guy 120
Towers, Constance 114
Tracy, Spencer 65, 125
Traver, Catherine 149
Tregouet, Yahn 146
Tripplehorn, Jean 46
The Truman Show 72–74
Trumbo, Dalton 108, 114
Tucci, Stanley 173
Turner, Lana 124
12 Angry Men 7, 9–10, 87, 95
2001: Space Odyssey 111

Unamuno, Miguel De 32
Under Fire 108

Under the Sand 89–90
The Usual Suspects 18
Utilitarianism 19–27, 43, 93, 109, 128, 153, 183–185

Valadon, Suzanne 147
van Gogh, Vincent 82
The Vanishing 12–13
Vega, Vladimir 140
von Sydow, Max 34, 99
von Trier, Lars 56

Wachowski, Andy 74
Wachowski, Larry 74
Wahlberg, Mark 166
Waking Life 12
Walken, Christopher 113
Walker, Alexander 111
Walker, Alice 78
Walters, Julie 69
war 104–114
Wargnier, Regis 169–170
Washington, Denzel 114, 122, 125, 156, 181
Washington, Fredi 124
Wasson, Craig 164
Watson, Emily 56–57
Watt, Richard, M. 107
Watts, Naomi 186–187
Wayne, John 114
We Are Not Afraid: The Story of Goodman, Schwerner and Chaney and the Civil Rights Campaign for Mississippi 118
Weaving, Hugo 75, 160
Weir, Peter 72, 90
Wender, Wim 60
Whale, James 160
Whale Rider 134, 147–148
What Dreams May Come 102
When Harry Met Sally 167–169
Whitaker, Forrest 18
Whose Life Is It Anyway? 92–94
Wiest, Dianne 34
Wild Man Blues 35
Wild Strawberries 101
Wilde 160
Williams, Michelle 156
Williams, Robin 114
Winfrey, Oprah 79
Winger, Debra 88, 102

Wings of Desire 60
Winslet, Kate 166
Winter Light 99
Wolf, Naomi 134
*The World's Religions: Our Great Wisdom
    Traditions* 52
Wyman, Jane 123

Ying, Ruocheng 53
Yojimbo 17
Yuelin, Zhao 30

Zahedi, Caveh 12
Zamachowski, Zbigniew 65
Zazvorkova, Stella 102
Zeffirelli, Franco 66
Zelig 35
Zhang, Ziyi 30
Zhao, Yuelin 30
Zindulke, Stanislav 102
Zinnemann, Fred 29
Ziyi, Zhang 30